MILITARY MODELLING GUIDE
TO MILITARY MODELLING

GUIDE TO
MILITARY MODELLING

KEN JONES

ARGUS BOOKS

Argus Books Limited
1 Golden Square
London W1R 3AB
England

ISBN 0 85242 904 5

Phototypesetting by Poole Typesetting (Wessex) Limited, Bournemouth
Printed and bound by L R Printing Services Ltd,
Manor Royal, Crawley, West Sussex, RH10 2QN, England.

CONTENTS

INTRODUCTION

From the many letters and telephone calls I receive as editor of the monthly hobby magazine *Military Modelling,* I find that a lot of the people who express interest, whether in painting figures or making military vehicles, simply do not know where to begin. In most cases this is due to there being nothing currently in print which explains, simply, what the hobby is all about. A plethora of alien terms is encountered by the beginner, and while no book of this size can fully explain every aspect, a beginner's guide has been sorely needed for some time.

Some ask why oil paints are used by figure painters — and must they use them too? The answer is no! Paint with what you like. No hard and fast rules should govern any pastime, but there should obviously be some guidelines for beginners, at least to enable them to understand the basic terminology and what it entails so that when they progress, they can understand what is meant by manufacturers' instructions and what authors of modelling features are really saying.

The purpose of this book is to *generalise* for the beginner on just what military modelling is. No examples of actual modelling projects are given, as this would 'localise' the theme far too much and not really be in step with the prime intention of offering a basic introduction to the subject.

Some of the photographs in the book are from the vast photo-files of *Military Modelling* magazine. Where the modeller is known he has been named, but this has not always been possible and it is to these modellers and the many younger modellers and beginners everywhere participating in this fascinating hobby that this book is respectfully dedicated. Day to day communication with modellers is perhaps the most satisfying part of editing a magazine, and such communication is the fuel for this book.

I would like to thank Linda Fox for typing the manuscript ... she was most helpful.

Ken Jones

1 SCALES AND THE MILITARY MODELLER

Scales are a necessary part of any modelling pursuit and a good working knowledge is essential if any sort of understanding is to be gained from the mass of unfamiliar data which initially tends to confuse the modeller.

Unfortunately there is very little standardisation on scales either by manufacturers or the model press. It is quite common to see a scale quoted as a ratio, a mixture of metric and imperial measure and a "borrowed" coding system from railway modelling — thus 1:76; 4mm = 1 foot; OO/HO.

As far as the military modeller is concerned, there are two situations where scales apply — figure and vehicle modelling — and these become important when entering models in competitions or when a collection of figures or vehicles, or both together in diorama form, is envisaged. In order to simplify matters somewhat, figures scales and vehicle scales will be explained separately but, where they are compatible, reference will be made.

Commercial availability also dictates popularity and segregation of models into various so-called 'popular scales' is common practice simply because much use can be made of kit parts. Any further additions or new ranges are, therefore, designed to these 'popular scales', particularly in the case of plastic model vehicle kits. However, figures, while following nominal scales, do diverge into many unusual and, in many cases 'one off' sizes, more by accident than design. Before listing the scales used in military modelling a basic explanation is necessary.

RATIOS

Scales are expressed as ratios for both figures and model vehicle kits, but mainly the latter. The ratio is simply an expression of relative size. For example, 1:35 means that the model is 1/35th the size of the real thing. If the model is one foot or one metre long the subject from which it is taken is 35 feet or 35 metres long. It doesn't matter which "units" are used for measuring — one unit on the model will still be represented by 35 on the real thing.

Modellers are still faced by plans which quote a ratio and have a bar scale in feet and sometimes a dual feet/metres scale is included. Other modellers 'brought' up with imperial measure do not always feel comfortable with metric measure and often convert freely between the two which gives rise to some model kits labelled, for example, 4mm = 1 foot, or 1:76 scale.

This is derived from converting the ratio thus:

$$\frac{1 \times 25.4 \times 12}{76} = 4\text{mm represents one foot.}$$

25.4 is the conversion factor for inches to millimetres.

Nominal dimensions
Heights in millimetres are the most commonly quoted model figure scales. These are not, for obvious reasons, used for vehicles whereas a ratio can be used for both.

Figure heights used to be expressed in inches some years ago, but are now exclusively quoted in millimetres. The model figure is measured from the ground to the top of the head, excluding head-dress. The most common or traditional military model figurine size is 54mm (2 inches) which is also sometimes referred to as 1:32 scale. The height is calculated on a "human form" of 5 feet 9 inches tall (1.75 metres) which is adopted as an average height. Obviously human heights and statures vary but rarely do designers "adjust" their model figures accordingly.

Figures in the larger scales, which are normally plastic construction kits, are indicated as ratios rather than nominal height, e.g. 1:9 and 1:12 scales. A list of common scales in use along with product availability is appended at the end of this chapter.

Other designations
Vehicles and figures in the smaller scales can bear the dimensional description more associated with model railways. These are OO (1:76 scale) and HO (1:87 scale). Often

Ratio	Nominal Figure height in mm. Based on average 5ft 9ins	Metric/ Imperial Millimetres equalling - 1 foot	Remarks
1:300	6	1	Z gauge (railway)
1:250	7	1.2	
1:200	9	1.5	
1:150	11.5	2	N
1:100	17.25	3	TT
1:96	18	3.2	
1:90	19	3.4	
1:87	20	3.5	H0
1:76	23	4	00
1:72	24	4.2	
1:58	30	5	
1:50	34.5	6	
1:48	36.5	6.3	$\frac{1}{4}$ scale
1:43	40	7	0 gauge (railway) International "Die Cast" scale – Solido tanks
1:40	44	7.6	
1:38	46	8	
1:35	50	8.7	
1:32	54.5	9.5	
1:30	58	10	60mm nominal – Historex figures
1:25	69.5	12	
1:24	73	12.7	75mm nominal
1:21	83	14.5	80mm nominal
1:20	87	15.2	90mm nominal
1:16	109.25	19	
1:10	175	30	
1:9	195	34	200 nominal
1:8	219	38	

(Note: Figures in metric/millimetres conversion and Figure heights are rounded off for convenience.)

the two are incorrectly lumped together as OO/HO to further add to the confusion. The origin of this unfortunate merger can be traced back some sixty years and relates to the smaller size and hence lack of motor space of British prototype locomotives compared with those of other countries.

Page 9 provides a descriptive table of the commoner scales the military modeller will encounter.

SCALES, SPACE AND COLLECTING

When most people take up modelling of any sort they do not as a rule adhere to any common scale. Later, 'specialising' in one particular scale is the normal state of affairs.

Whatever scale or scales a modeller adopts is often dictated by the immediate domestic environment. Big tanks, lorries and figures around 100mm tall take up a lot of storage space and no one really likes to have the fruits of their labours hidden away in boxes in the attic when they should be on display.

Selecting an 'ideal' scale is purely a personal choice but it is worth considering any prohibiting factors that may emerge as you progress. While it's a good idea – and good practice – to try your hand at painting different sizes of figurines, for example, it should be remembered just where you will keep them all.

POPULAR SCALES

Although you can make models to any size, scales are usually dictated by commercial output and availability: the following are some of the most popular.

1:87 scale A popular scale in continental Europe, equating to a figure height of 20mm,and often labelled as 'HO', which is the model railway scale.

Model vehicle availability, with figures too, is very good from Roco Minitanks, Faller and Preiser. As always, confusion occurs and some British manufacturers list 20mm figures as 1:76 scale which is not surprising when one considers the British "manufacturing approach" to railway scales and gauges. Airfix listed their 1:76 scale figures as 20mm.

Scale in collecting figures is important for display purposes. These Benassi figures are, from left to right, 54mm, 90mm and 80mm.

1:76 scale Popularised by Airfix in the early 1960s and based on the British model railway scale of OO or, as often labelled, "4mm = 1 foot scale". This is a scale rigidly adhered to by British AFV scratchbuilders for whom its popularity is promoted and kept alive. Figures should scale out at around 23mm plus.

It is a good scale for scratchbuilders and for large collections and the space-conscious. Figure modellers will find the size a 'little too small', although some do collect and convert plastic commercial figures in this scale.

1:72 scale The most popular model aircraft scale. A large variety of figures and vehicle kits are widely available, mainly from Japan, although Italian manufacturers have added many more. Some well-detailed figures intended for war games, moulded in soft, polythene-type plastic from the Italian maker ESCI, are most attractive to collectors.

1:58 scale An unfamiliar ratio, but one that equates to the figure height of 30mm and a scale once popular with figure painters but which now has limited appeal. However, Phoenix Model Developments, Tradition, and others still produce 30mm figures. Vehicles are not available in great numbers.

The vulcanised two-part rubber mould used for casting white metal figures. This one belongs to Chota Sahib of Brighton.

Below, centrifugal casting machines with the thermostatically-controlled melting pots between. Chota Sahib of Brighton.

1:48 scale Also known as 'quarter scale' and another popular model aircraft scale, there are not as many model vehicle kits in this scale as 10-15 years ago. Figures are mainly produced for aircraft ground crews, aircrew and the like. Figures in this scale are around 37mm high.

1:43 scale Not much, if anything, in the way of vehicle construction kits in this scale, which is the diecast vehicle scale. The French company, Solido, did produce some tanks in 1:43 scale. Also listed as 7mm scale or O gauge model railway scale, the figures are 40mm tall and military types are not available in any quantity or variety.

1:35 scale One of the most popular military vehicle kit scales introduced during the early 1960s with imports from Japan. Figures, around 50mm tall, are available but are limited to WWII period to the present day. A good choice of vehicle kits of all periods plus resin and white metal figure ranges from Japanese, French and Italian manufacturers.

1:32 scale A very popular model figure scale which is more commonly referred to as 54mm scale, the height of the figurine. Vehicles to this scale are not as numerous as 1:35 scale. However, Airfix flirted with making vehicles in this scale. There are some white metal vehicles which are expensive. There are more figures produced in 54mm scale than any other. Practically every figure manufacturer produces models in this scale and there is much to choose from.

1:30 scale Vehicle scale adopted by Russian and other Eastern countries for plastic kits which are available only in limited numbers in the West. This scale is also the size, around 58mm tall, adopted by Historex for their plastic figure models — mainly all Napoleonic wars period. *Note:* Some white metal figures are produced to 60mm and 65mm scales, probably more from 'over estimation' on a 54mm figure by the sculptor than by design. However, 65mm scale seems to have established itself with some manufacturers, and will therefore probably become accepted and standardised.

1:24 scale The nominal 75mm figure scale, also termed half-inch scale. Closely allied to 1:25 scale for vehicles and some

A modelling demonstration in progress. John Tassell shows the art of converting white metal figures with the soldering iron.

plastic figures from Japanese manufacturers. Good variety in 75mm white metal figures mainly from British figure designers.

1:20 scale Not many vehicles in this scale, but plenty of figures where 87mm equals the height of a 5 feet 9 inches tall person, although this "rounds off" to 90mm, a very popular larger figure scale.

Larger scales Some plastic figure construction kits, from Airfix, Tamiya and Imai to 1:12 scale and ESC1 in 1:9 scale are eagerly sought, built and converted by modellers. These are plastic injection moulded kits of a hollow construction and thus easy to convert, especially by beginners. These figures are ideal to practise on.

Give plenty of thought and attention to scales, what they mean and why we use them. Learn to use and understand scales, as in the next chapter the use of drawings will be discussed. You will then not be deterred from, say, building a military vehicle in 1:35 scale when you have a drawing in 1:40 scale and know how to convert the dimensions.

2 RESEARCH

Research work by modellers is just as interesting and often more time-consuming than actually painting a figure, building a tank kit or constructing a diorama.

Why do we need to find out more about the things we model? The answer is simple — to improve our standards and techniques and to ensure realism and accuracy. However, modelling is fun and detailed research should always be taken in its correct context.

Modellers have been known to allow research to overtake their modelling pursuits and, in many cases, collecting research material can totally oust the basic initial pastime. Both aspects are good fun and, though research can become more mentally stimulating or frustrating, it should never be allowed to supersede the prime task of producing the model.

GATHERING MATERIAL

There is nothing more frustrating than to build, say, a model vehicle and perpetuate a common mistake, incorporated by the manufacturer, which everyone else knows about except yourself. Basic research, and the most basic is verbal communication with modellers, can avoid such errors. Alternatively, a visit to the local public library can provide the wherewithal to ascertain any instructional or material mistakes.

Be on the lookout for anything useful, not only material on current projects, but anything you consider worthwhile. Become a hoarder of everything pertaining to your hobby.

Museums
Military museums offer a wealth of information and they often have publications on sale. Most larger towns and cities

have regimental museums or similar establishments in addition to the national museums in the capital and elsewhere. Visits to all such establishments should be encouraged whenever possible, after first making an appointment if necessary. Some military museums issue readers' tickets for researchers, so check before attending. The location of regimental museums can usually be found in the local library. However, there is a publication available which describes all United Kingdom regimental museums, and details of this are given in the appendices.

Official Bodies

The Ministry of Defence and foreign embassies are good sources of information. Public relations officers and military attaches are usually very helpful and responsive to reasonable requests, or can put you in touch with the appropriate contact who will supply the information. Remember, security does cover a good slice of military matters so do not expect information that is normally unavailable, particularly where equipment is concerned. However, uniforms and suchlike are subjects where information is readily made available.

Unlike museums, material from official bodies is normally supplied free of charge. The addresses of embassies (within the United Kingdom, for example, all in London) can be found in the telephone directory. It is surprising how many modellers ignore these excellent and often untapped sources of material.

Military shows and open days, also sources of prime material, should be visited whenever possible. A notebook and camera are essential on such visits and it is interesting to note how quickly you amass much useful information. Even the 'Cavalry Old Comrades' parade, a yearly event in London's Hyde Park, will offer much in the way of British army dress uniforms; excellent reference for figure painters. You may not need it at the moment, but you may in the future. Remember, what you get today will help tomorrow.

Libraries

Public libraries are fine institutions, coupled to the central library system operating in the U.K. Virtually every book in print, and many out of print, can be obtained on application.

Join your local library and use the facilities offered for your research as an aid to your modelling.

Public Records
Public records offices are useful when researching obscure information on military units and their uniforms, structure and so on. Access to records is usually by appointment to the office concerned and it is wise to be specific in your requests so that the staff can give you maximum help. Know exactly what you're looking for and, before you begin, acquire as many leads as possible. You may have to wait a long time for research material to be delivered and as in some records offices a reader's ticket may be necessary, check before you visit.

Press agencies
Good photographs and information can be got from newspaper offices and the many press agencies. Fees are charged — often expensive — by press agencies for private requests but much excellent material is available from these sources. Foreign countries' press agencies are 'goldmines' to the diligent researcher. Advance appointments are required if you wish to go through records and fees are charged for material.

FILING SYSTEMS

It's a complete waste of your time if you do not collate and store any information you acquire in a manner where you can locate that information quickly.

The most obvious method of storing material is a scrapbook or in some cases a type of file card index. Written information is best put on a card system, and photographs and cuttings pasted into a scrapbook. Often the two can be used together and cross-referenced for ease of operation.

As a beginner it's best to start as you mean to continue. There is nothing worse than to have a lot of material jumbled up without any order and where you have to spend a lot of time searching for what you want — or even to realise that you didn't really have what you're searching for in the first place — so plan ahead.

A card index system is simple to begin and to maintain.

Index cards are cheap and available in different sizes and should be stored alphabetically in boxes made specially for them or in suitably sized card boxes. Smaller photographs can be stuck to index cards for a more compact system, but if larger magazine cuttings are to be stored they can't really be incorporated in a standard card index system. These are better stuck into a scrapbook using a 'stick' type adhesive, such as Pritt, which is clean and non-staining.

Military modellers who paint figures or build vehicles need a lot of illustrative reference — uniform types, colour information, badges and the like, or close-up details of vehicles. If this is 'double-sided' with material on both sides of a page removed from a magazine, store these in envelopes — unfolded — in manila folders or wallets, or in the transparent document wallets on sale in stationers.

As the reference material or library grows some form of index system will have to be devised.

With the growth in popularity of home computers a whole new world of storing information presents itself to modellers. Storage programs can be purchased or devised for solid information or index purposes.

A CAMERA

Most people have a camera of some description. Modellers should try to use a camera whenever possible to accumulate as much pictorial reference as possible.

Postcards bought at museums and at military open days yield a superb source of accurate uniform research . . . and they're cheap to buy.

There are simple rules to follow when photographing for record purposes. If what you need to photograph is in a military museum, make sure that photography is permitted — or if at a show or military parade, ensure you do not obstruct anyone when obtaining your pictures. Also, do not photograph anything you are told not to. Such irresponsible actions can spoil things for everyone else.

COLOUR AND THE MODELLER

The modeller must know about colour and what constitutes it. Figure modellers must know about the difference between 'red' and 'crimson', for instance, or between 'Prussian Blue and 'French Blue'. Interpretation of colour is difficult, because we must reduce "to scale" any paint colours we use and experience is the only yardstick. It's no use trying to match colours to actual examples, despite all the "hot air" expounded by so many self-styled experts. Original sources can only be used as guidance — and guidance alone — for colour matching on any miniature subject.

Remember also that uniforms, especially old surviving examples, fade so are not really reliable sources anyway. What it all boils down to is that the modeller must use his own judgement. It is an indisputable fact that any two modellers would paint khaki in two different shades. The difference may be subtle, but different all the same.

This holds true for vehicles. Fading and weathering all take their toll and, unless a 'factory finish' is desired, which never looks realistic anyway, some measure of intelligent interpretation is needed.

Scale colour has been mentioned and this is simply the "reduction" process making the colour appear lighter overall. You could not, for example, paint a model with the exact shade, or the same paint for that matter, as that used on the real thing. For a start, it would be too dark and this is where the colour has to be lightened and artistic licence taken. Again experience will show what is right and what "feels" and "looks" right.

Colour pictures printed in magazines are not suitable for exact comparisons, whereas a colour print or slide would be nearer, but only if correctly exposed. Try altering your exposure on one subject and see what happens!

There are far too many myths surrounding so-called exact colour matching and a lot of rubbish talked about colour itself. If it looks right compared with the real thing then you've succeeded — if not, try again.

PLANS AND SCALE DRAWINGS

Unlike the figure modeller and painter the vehicle modeller is a great user of plans or scale drawings. By the very nature of the subject — a tank, armoured car, truck, car or whatever — the modeller must at some time refer to a drawing or a

Good clear plans are needed for model making. This plan by the author shows the four basic views needed, side, plan, front and rear elevations.

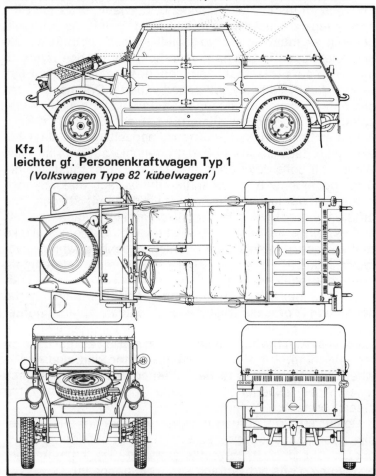

Kfz 1
leichter gf. Personenkraftwagen Typ 1
(Volkswagen Type 82 ´kübelwagen´)

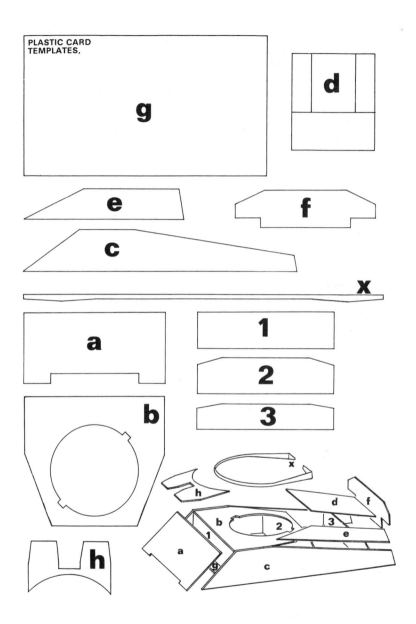

PLASTIC CARD TEMPLATES,

Parts needed to build the hull of a 1:35 scale Sherman M4A2 tank made up from a four-view plan by the author. The key at bottom right shows how they all fit together. This hull replaced the one in a kit and was cut out and assembled from 30 thou plastic card.

photograph to improve upon the kit under construction. Later, when attempting a scratchbuilt model, a scale drawing is a necessity and without it making an accurate model would be virtually impossible.

Always follow one basic rule when working from drawings, and that is to take measurements from the dimensions shown in all views — never from one view only. Also, observe how sloping surfaces are not equal in all views. This may sound obvious, but many people do make this most basic of errors, some repeatedly.

Drawing your own plans
It is almost impossible to teach anyone to produce scale drawings from a book. However, it is possible to pass on some pointers which should help anyone with a modicum of artistry to feel more confident about producing a drawing.

If you have access to the subject a drawing is, of course, much easier. All basic measurements should be taken and if the subject is large an assistant does help. Photograph the subject from both sides, front and rear, and with as much detail as you consider necessary. Where possible, include a measuring rod marked off in feet or metres in the photos and ensure it is always parallel to the camera. This will be invaluable for the finer details. If you only have photographs to work from you will not be able to obtain a completely accurate drawing but with care you should achieve a passable and workable set of elevations. Only very few drawings are the result of measuring and examining the real thing.

For working from photographs you must also have a set of dimensions or, at least an accurate overall length, and from the photographs calculate the other measurements. Transfer these to a drawing starting with a side view.

Adequate working drawings can be made in pencil on paper. Project the side elevation into front, rear and plan views. Initially, stick to elementary straight line work. With a wider availability of photocopying facilities it is possible to draw your plans to a larger scale and photo-reduce them to the scale in which you model. Finally, produce templates of each part whenever possible and use these to mark out. If you can join a local model club, do so — there is usually someone who can help you to draw plans and get you started.

3 TOOLS AND MATERIALS

Almost every pastime or hobby requires some form of basic tool kit and military modelling is no exception. The basic toolkit is in no way sophisticated or costly but it can in time grow into quite a collection as extra tools are added. Materials used in military modelling are as varied as those used by other scale modellers of, for example, aircraft, ships and railways. Although not 'every day' materials, they are widely available both from model shops and by mail order.

TOOLS

Accurate marking out, particularly for vehicle modellers, is very important, and therefore pens, pencils and scribers should be chosen carefully.

A good quality steel rule marked off in metric and imperial units, will perform a dual function — measuring for marking out and as a straight edge for cutting. Do not use a plastic rule as a straight edge guide when cutting out materials, because one slip with a sharp knife and you could ruin the rule and your fingers. Start as you mean to go on and never

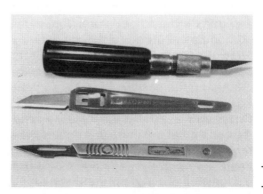

Modelling knives are important and should be one of, if not *the,* first tools bought by the modeller. Top is a heavy duty X-Acto, middle a disposable Stanley and bottom a Swann Morton Series 3 Scalpel.

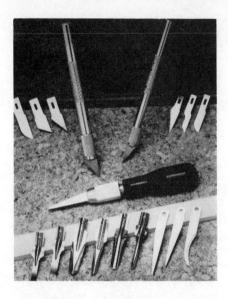

Comprehensive range of knives and gouges in the Xcelite range from Toolmail.

use a plastic rule as a cutting guide. Invest in a steel rule — six inch and 1 foot types are ideal.

An asset, although not absolutely necessary, is a steel set-square for marking out perfect right angles from a known straight edge.

Pencils, especially the automatic clutch type with a fine lead, are ideal for marking out. Points 0.3mm are available, although a point of 0.5mm is suitable for general work. The fine tips of these pencils are designed for use with a straight edge and, unlike conventional wooden/graphite pencils, retain their points at the touch of a button. Technical pens such as Rotring and Staedler are useful for many tasks, though not essential.

A compass and dividers will be required for circle drawing and transferring dimensions from plan to material. A combined compass cutting tool is also an asset and is mentioned later. An engineer's steel scriber is useful for marking out plastic card because it is possible to score and break this material quite easily.

Cutting tools
A good modelling knife or a scalpel is essential. There are no real substitutes and razor blades and suchlike should not be used. Two knives are needed — one for normal light work, e.g. cutting out parts from flat sheet, cutting small parts and

small carving tasks and one with a thicker and stouter blade for heavier work. The latter is especially helpful for heavy carving on tough materials.

Choose your knives carefully — the X-Acto range is very good and versatile with a large choice of blade types and handles. Swann Morton scalpels are of good quality and will last a lifetime with only the blades, which are reasonably cheap, to replace for each model. A number 3 handle is the most suitable and has a large selection of blades to fit it. Model shops, local or mail order, craft material stockists or art suppliers are good sources for scalpels.

'Razor' or slitting saws, as produced by X-Acto, are extremely useful for cutting both plastics and wood but they are not really suited to harder materials such as metals. Although razor saws will cut white metal effectively any thick pieces will cause the saw to bind and the teeth to clog. A coping or piercing saw is a much better tool for cutting and converting white metal figures.

A compass cutter, mentioned in the section on marking-out equipment, is a useful piece of equipment. Perhaps the best known variant is that made by Olfa of Japan. Working in a similar manner to a conventional compass, an angled cutting blade is fitted instead of a lead.

By continuous scribing, perfect circles can be cut from card or plastic card and this is useful for making up, for example, wheels from laminated sections of plastic card.

Snips or nippers are very handy for plastic kit modellers as they enable kit parts to be cleanly removed from the sprues. They are handier than a knife and safer than twisting parts away, which can lead to damage. Ordinary household

Small nippers are recommended for removing plastic kit parts from their runners or sprues.

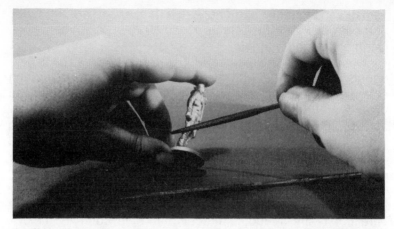

Small files, known frequently as 'Swiss' files, are invaluable for working on white metal figures.

scissors have their place, though they should never be used for accurate cutting — always leave this to the knife. However, they are useful for rough cutting out of card and thin plastic sheet.

Abrasives

Sanding down and cleaning off to a clean finish is a task that takes time and practice, with both metal files and abrasive papers.

The military modeller needs files and plenty of them. There are three basic types of small files — needle, riffler and warding files.

Files clog easily when filing white metal, so to avoid this put talcum powder on the teeth before you begin. Plastic can be removed with a wire brush, which can also remove large white metal deposits, though once white metal clogs in a file it's very difficult to remove. Files come in six different

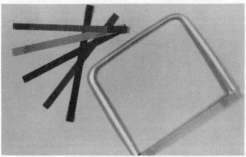

A superb idea from the United States is the Flex-I-File. Very good for sanding rounded surfaces because it virtually eliminates any 'flattening'.

Scotchbrite abrasive is superb for plastic and white metal. This pack is sold by Proops Bros. as model railway track cleaning pads.

shapes: round, square, three-square, flat, hand and half round. Needle files do not usually have handles and are about 5½in. (140mm) long, whereas warding files have wooden handles, are larger overall and are about 7in (178mm) long. Small riffler files are versatile, about six inches long and are double-ended with curved, pointed and shaped ends enabling filing of hard-to-reach places. Although they are expensive they tend to be better than straight-bladed needle files due to their curved blades. Made of chrome vanadium, files will last a long time if cared for and reserved for only light work such as modelling. Do not use them for heavy domestic tasks for which they are not designed. A rat or mouse tail flexible file is a round-section file and is useful for enlarging holes and other suchlike. It can be made to bend slightly.

Abrasives such as "sandpaper", (which is a generic term) emery and wet-and-dry, together with Scotchbrite, are all the modeller needs for general work. Wire wool is handy on white

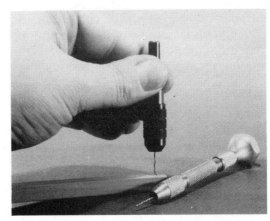

Two types of 'Pin Vice'. These will not only hold drill bits but can be used for holding minute parts during soldering, etc.

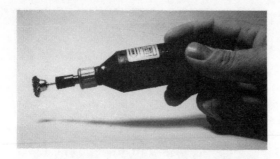

Minicraft's 'Prince' drill fitted with a wire cup brush for cleaning up white metal castings.

metal figures, as is a fibre glass brush. "Sandpaper" is really glasspaper and is intended for wood whereas emery paper is stronger and is for use on metal. Wet and dry papers are made from silicon carbide and are intended to be used with water which acts as a lubricant when sanding surfaces and helps to stop the grit clogging. As the name suggests, these can be used dry too.

Scotchbrite is a type of plastic "wire wool" and is excellent for smoothing and polishing plastic. It is produced by the 3M Company and reasonably priced.

Drills

The word "drill" to the layman, if applied to modelling in miniature, conjures up visions of mini-motorised drills (see under Power Tools) with micro-twist drill bits. While there is a place for motorised drills many experienced modellers, especially those working with plastics, would rather use a small hand drill or pin vice — also known as a pin chuck, which is a more accurate description. A pin vice is also a small hand vice! Motorised tools, unless a speed control is fitted, tend to melt plastic rather than drill it cleanly.

White metal can be difficult to drill for precisely the same reason — friction causes heat and the drill binds. Really it's a matter of experimenting on various materials.

The pin chuck, which is usually supplied with different sized collets, is rotated between the fingers and it ensures control especially on very small parts 1/16in and below, such as drilling out plastic rod section to represent a gun barrel. Twist drills are available in all sizes from those thinner than a household pin up to the standard DIY sizes and above. To kit yourself out with everything would, of course, be totally impractical — financially! Furthermore, small drills are not widely on sale and tend to be stocked by specialist suppliers.

The "normal" range of high speed twist drills runs from 1/16in. to about $\frac{1}{4}$in. or, metric, around $1\frac{1}{2}$mm or 2mm upwards to 8mm. Quality depends on the price you pay but anything smaller and the price goes up. Also the mortality rate of small drills can be high in inexperienced hands and anything below a 1mm twist drill should be used very cautiously in a mini power tool. If metal is worked on continuously, twist drills soon become blunt.

Protect your eyes when drilling with mini-power tools because small drills can turn into small unguided missiles if they snap during drilling. Protective goggles are cheap and, although you may never have such an accident, always put safety first.

Supporting the work

It is important to grip the material securely whilst you work on it. Even when painting a single white metal figure it must be firmly supported, leaving all-round access for your paint brush or whatever.

The conventional vice is very handy and there are specialist modellers' vices now available. One of the most useful is a plastic suction vice which clamps to a clean, smooth working surface by creating a vacuum in a nylon sucker on its undersurface. This is done by swinging a lever down to lock it. It is eminently suited to light modelling work. Small metal vices that clamp onto the workbench, a board or the kitchen table are reasonably priced and very useful.

A home-made clamp can be made by fixing spring clothes pegs to a wooden block which, along with rubber bands, can hold painted parts to dry.

Small plastic suction base vice as marketed by Proops Bros. The suction base will adhere to any clean smooth surface.

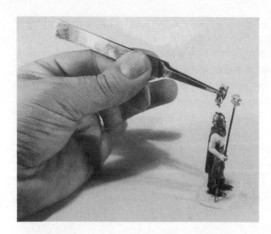

Good quality tweezers are an essential modelling aid.

Metal 'G' clamps by Faber and available from most DIY stores are an invaluable modelling aid.

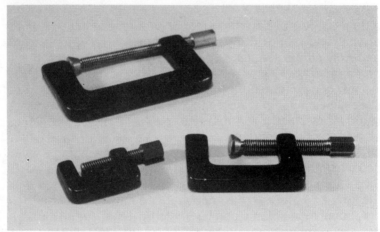

'Helping Hands' will hold any work in place for soldering, glueing, detailing, etc., at any angle. This one is a very reasonably priced tool from Proops Bros.

Pliers, especially the smaller varieties made for smaller work and modelling, should be added to the tool kit as soon as possible. Snipe and round nose types, including a pair with side cutters, are all you need to begin with. Wire is difficult to bend, especially if it's the harder type, and pliers are just the ticket to handle it.

All clamps, from the small pin vice to larger engineering types, are useful, though the pin vice is the best to buy first. Plastic modelmakers' clamps, which are held together by nothing more complicated than an elastic band, are cheap but very useful.

Metal screw "G" clamps are good for holding heavier materials, especially where soldering is being done, and they can double as heat sinks in some cases, keeping heat away from previously soldered joints.

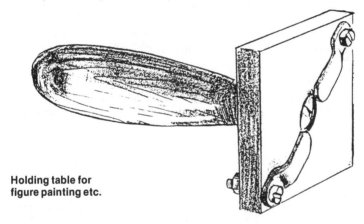

Holding table for figure painting etc.

"Helping Hands" is a useful piece of equipment which consists of a heavy, cast metal base with a central adjustable bar mounted on a ball and socket joint with, in turn, ball and socket joints with crocodile clips on both ends. This assembly will grip really fine work while you carry out the necessary operations on it.

Tweezers are the modeller's friend and the military modeller needs more than one pair. Avoid the cheap pressed metal types sold as part of a tool kit and buy a good pair, or better still, buy two or more pairs — you won't regret it. Fine points with straight and angled tips are most helpful with small parts. The tweezers must be comfortable to hold and well constructed with accurate points, about five to six inches long.

A most useful aid for holding figures for painting, once available commercially, is very easy to make at home and is shown on page 31. Figures, plastic or white metal, up to 65mm, can be held securely and all that is needed is a handle, a flat "table" about $1\frac{1}{2}$". × $1\frac{1}{2}$"., two small bolts with wing nuts and two metal strips — you could use brass turnbuttons of the types used in music and 'cigarette box making'.

The "table" is fixed to the handle — a wooden or plastic file handle makes a good one — and the strips positioned at opposite corners. The figure's base is held by the strips and the drawing explains it all.

Motor tools

Motor tools operating on a 12 volt supply were mentioned earlier in the section on drills and they are a tremendous boon to the military modeller. Not only do they accept drills, but also slitting discs, saws, burrs and many other attachments. Avoid cheap motor tools and go for a good branded name. Cheap tools vibrate and are not easy to control even with speed controls, and the motors can burn out much quicker than a better model.

Vertical drill presses and stands are available to hold the drill and can be added as your power tool kit grows. If possible try the tools before you buy. A wire cup and circular-type brush fitted to a power tool is a time-saving device for cleaning up white metal figures and it gets into all the inaccessible places. However, do not overdo any wire brush work as, although it is a labour-saver, it can also destroy some of the fine engraving on the model.

Later, with practice, engraving tips in the mini drill will enable you to experience a whole new approach on detailing white metal figures.

Soldering Irons

As with most tools, soldering irons do need a lot of practice. Novices rarely achieve perfect soldered joints intially and many do not progress past the first steps, deciding it's too much bother and resorting to some of the modern types of glues rather than persevering with hot iron, flux and solder. Soldering is simply the joining of two metal surfaces with the application of heat and a liquid metal (the solder) whose flow is controlled in and along the joint with flux.

Soldering kit for white metal. Carr's 70 low temperature solder and flux with the Litesold EC50 tacking iron. The brush is for applying the liquid flux.

Soldering is not difficult if you remember some very basic rules. All joints to be soldered must be scrupulously cleaned, the correct flux selected, iron capable of delivering the required heat and, if possible, solder and the iron should be brought to the joint together.

Military modellers, especially white metal figure painters, will find that a soldered joint is superior to a glued type. In addition, the very nature of low-melt solder enables it to act as a filler, so dispensing with the need for fillers on joints which are less than perfect. AFV modellers also, may need to replace fine plastic, or overscale and incorrect items, with wire or metal rod, and such assemblies benefit from soldered construction.

For white metal, a special low-melt solder is needed plus the appropriate flux and, of course, a low-temperature soldering iron, because most white metal alloys used in model figure casting melt around and over 95°C. Therefore, the solder must have a lower melting point and most commercially available solders liquefy around 70°C. Properties of these solders, and they are simply *lower* melting point alloys, vary, but those for modelling will have gap-filling capabilities which is to the modeller's advantage.

Flux used for white metal is a clear organic type, active at low temperatures but it is corrosive if left on the soldered joints. It must always be washed away with warm water. This holds true for almost all fluxes and it is good practice whenever possible to flush all joints after soldering. Also, avoid inhaling any vapour given off from soldered joints, as they are not only unpleasant but also can be harmful.

Soldering irons with some sort of heat control are the most suitable, and those operating with a bi-metal control slip are ideal. A standard iron can be modified with some form of voltage control wired into its power supply but this is something that should be left to a qualified electrician or someone experienced in electrics. However, commercially available devices for temperature control are available.

Probably the most suitable iron for white metal work is a conversion to a photographic tacking iron as assembled by Litesold for Carr's Modelling Products. Rated at 50 watts, the regulated tip temperature is 70°C maintained 100 times a second via solid state electronics in the handle. The makers claim accuracy to within less than one degree.

When soldering many joints in a close area it will be found that due to heat transmission through metal, the iron's application can cause previously soldered joints to become unsoldered! This can happen, for example, on wire used for a vehicle tilt frame of the type used to support a canvas sheet over the rear open body of a military truck. A heat sink is the answer. This is basically a piece or pieces of metal secured around a joint to block or divert the heat from already soldered joints in the vicinity. A crocodile clip of the type used in electric circuitry is the most convenient method to use, because of its easy application and removal and its good heat conduction. For a larger sink, crocodile clips can be used to clamp a sheet of metal in place.

When using irons other than low temperature types it is advisable to employ some form of heat sink for the tip while it is in use over long periods. Conducting heat away from the soldering iron's tip or bit will prolong the tip's life and enable its easy removal, preventing it from becoming "heat sealed" into the iron and thereby rendering it useless as a unit, for the sake of replacing the bit. A large block of metal for the tip to rest on is ideal, and any heavy cast iron base would suffice as long as heat is able to flow from the tip to be dispersed through the "sink".

Always use the correct soldering iron for the job. It's pointless trying a small iron designed for repairing printed circuits on a large mass such as white metal — even if the tip temperatures are low. It just won't work!

The Pyrogravure

The pyrogravure is a very useful tool for modellers who do most, if not all, of their work in plastic. The pen-shaped pyrogravure has a needle tip and operates on a 4.5 volt supply so it's safe and will not burn the fingers if the tip is accidentally touched.

Working from a combined mains plug transformer, the pyrogravure is easy to use and the modeller will soon become proficient in its use. It melts most plastics but is best on the polystyrene types; ABS plastics can be worked, but not as easily.

For texturing — melting the surface of plastic — many techniques are possible e.g. hair on figures and horses will certainly benefit from the pyrogravure's use, as will battle damage on plastic vehicle models. The anti-magnetic paste, *zimmerit,* applied to German tanks during WW2 can be cut into plastic surfaces with a pyrogravure, giving a most realistic finish in most scales except the very large.

The single-heat type is all the modeller should need under normal circumstances although for heavier work vari-heat models are available. Designed for wood and leather burning — or "poker work" — these pyrogravures are supplied with different tips to enable a variety of cuts and marks to be made. Although a little on the large side for "small scale modellers", they can be most useful for work on model buildings, large scale vehicles and scenic model terrain. Such pyrography sets are more expensive than the single-heat type.

Magnifying glasses

Under normal conditions a magnifying glass is not needed for modelling purposes but wearers of spectacles and those whose eyes are "not as good as they used to be" may need some form of assistance.

Stand magnifiers will aid painting of small scale figurines, though "working under the glass" does take some getting used to. It is not as easy to work under a glass as it is with the naked eye. Consider the length of the paint brush handle — invariably it fouls the magnifying lens if this is not mounted at an appropriate distance or the work, in relation to the lens, is badly placed, a fault of co-ordination which must be mastered before a comfortable relationship with a stand magnifier can be made.

Small magnifying lenses with suction pads for attaching to spectacles, or clip-on types will be the answer to many modellers' needs. Such optical devices are not cheap but if you need some form of clip-on magnifying lens seek advice from a registered optician, particularly if you intend attaching it to spectacles.

Jewellers', watchmakers' or toolmakers' loupes (eye-cup type magnifiers) are not really suitable for the modeller, especially for long period usage. Although they are reasonable in price, gripping such a device in one eye for long periods will become tedious.

Illuminated magnifiers are expensive, although a lot of figure modellers use them for close work such as painting faces on small scale figures or for painting flat figures. If you become used to working with a glass, fine — but if you don't need one to begin with, even better.

MATERIALS

The materials used by military modellers fall into four basic groups: plastics, metals, woods and paper or card.

PLASTICS

There are thousands of different plastics in general use and many of them are used by modellers today. They all have similar properties and fall into two groups — *thermoplastics* which can be melted down, thus retaining plastic characteristics, and *thermoset* which, once set, cannot be reduced to their original state.

Polystyrene

Plastics of the polystyrene type are the most commonly encountered. "Plastic kits" are moulded in polystyrene as are figures, "plastic card" sheets used for scratch building and parts for conversions.

Polystyrene is brittle and in order to ensure a small amount of elasticity rubber polymers are introduced. In this form polystyrene is known as "high impact". Its working temperature when it becomes fluid for injection moulding is around 75°C.

Plastic card is the general everyday term for sheets of

polystyrene, extruded into varying thicknesses, .010 — .060 inch, in .010 divisions. This can be scored, i.e. cut half through then snapped along the line to produce a clean cut. It can be drilled, carved and moulded by heat forming or vacuformed with appropriate equipment.

Polystyrene sheet comes in various colours and is also embossed in useful patterns such as brick and stone work, planking, corrugated, etc. Polystyrene rod and tube are commercially available too.

Polystyrene can be moulded as clear sheet but it must be in its original brittle state (i.e. no rubber added and therefore not high impact) for clarity. By gas expansion into a lower density cellular form expanded polystyrene foam is produced.

Polystyrene can be glued with liquid or polystyrene cements which consist of polystyrene dissolved in solvents such as ethylene dichloride or carbon tetrachloride.

ABS (Acrylobutyl Styrene)
ABS is similar to polystyrene in appearance but it is a more expensive medium of high impact strength. It can be treated in the same way as polystyrene and produces excellent injection mouldings of thinner gauge. It is also available in sheet form and as clear sheet, and lots of different shapes and mouldings are produced by "Plastruct", a company specialising in ABS production for model makers. ABS can, like polystyrene, be joined with a solution of ABS and a solvent such as ethyl isobutyl ketone. ABS can be stuck to polystyrene with this solvent though polystyrene glues are not successful in joining ABS plastics. ABS melts at around the same temperatures as polystyrene.

Acrylic ("Perspex")
"Perspex" is the trade name ("Plexiglass" in the US) for acrylic plastics and, although expensive, clear acrylic can be used by modellers for display cases and scenic modellers for representing water where its surface can be worked with a solvent or heat to produce ripples, etc. Acrylic can be moulded and needs its own cement or solvent to stick it. The thinner acrylic is, the more brittle it becomes.

Polythene
Polythene (or more correctly polyethylene) is used for

moulding figures, normally found in the popular scales 1:32, 1:76 and 1:72. It is a soft plastic with a "greasy" feel and is practically impossible to paint or glue together. In fact, the action of oil based enamel paints on polythene figures tends to produce a surface hardening which makes the material become brittle in the long term. Although resistant to solvents sticking it, it "soaks in" oils used in paints! It can be sealed — in the case of figurines, by coating with watered down PVA glues which dry onto the figure and shrink into a protective coat which will accept all known model paints without gradual deterioration.

It is virtually impossible to glue polystyrene, and any successful conversion work on figures must be made with a very sharp knife blade and joints reinforced with pins or similar before the completed conversion is coated with diluted PVA glue as a primer.

Polythene has a lower melting point than polystyrene at around 50°C – 60°C depending on its density.

Expanded Polystyrene

Best known for its use as a packaging material, expanded polystyrene can be adapted by the modeller mainly for scenic work. Being very light it is useful for making hills and ground work and, to a limited extent, buildings.

Consisting of gas-expanded polystyrene cells, the material is not easy to cut, although a very fine "saw" type blade will produce a clean cut. For finished work a hot wire cutter is best. These are powered by a battery and operate on about 4.5 - 6 volts and can easily be made from a frame of wood or metal with a wire stretched between. Of course, if the frame is metal the wire needs to be insulated from it. Use the thinnest wire possible for the cutter. Sticking expanded polystyrene must be done with water-based adhesives, because most other solvents simply melt it. The same with paints! Use only water-based types.

Resins

Resins are thermoset plastics. By mixing two agents they eventually produce, by chemical action, a rigid plastic substance which before setting can be poured into a mould or former to produce copies of a master model.

Two types will be found in use — a polyester type, which is the most common, and a polyurethane variety.

Polyester resins are brittle and any inconsistency in mixing causes a less than satisfactory result. Also the resin is difficult to cut and will not mould into thin parts very easily. Many small scale military vehicles are moulded in polyester resin. Opacity, colour and bulk are added to polyester by adding powder and the resin is made to harden by adding a catalyst (methyl ethyl ketone peroxide) to the manufacturer's directions.

Polyurethane resins are not as common as polyesters but they are much easier to use and more expensive. They are usually two-part liquid types with no powders to add for opacity. Both components are roughly the consistency of milk, the resin containing the filler. Normally mixed in 50 - 50 proportions, and being easy to mix, a type with a short "pot life" (i.e. before hardening commences) will produce mouldings more quickly than polyester types.

Resins work better during moulding if some form of de-gassing equipment is available to eliminate air bubbles. Such things are usually beyond the average modeller and care should be taken during pouring. Polyester resins seem to be, perhaps because of thicker consistencies, more prone to air bubbles than polyurethanes.

Silicone rubbers of the room temperature vulcanising (RTV) types are ideal for making moulds in which to cast

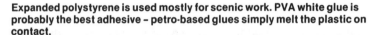

Expanded polystyrene is used mostly for scenic work. PVA white glue is probably the best adhesive – petro-based glues simply melt the plastic on contact.

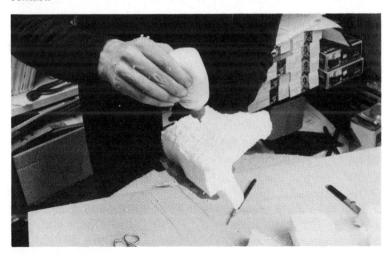

resins. Polyurethane resins are thin enough to spin in centrifugal casting machines too.

Polyurethane resins, unlike polyesters, can be drilled, carved and stuck together with conventional plastic cements.

METALS

All military modellers should familiarise themselves with the metals used for casting model soldiers. These alloys we know colloquially as "white metals"; brass and nickel silver sheets used for etchings are now finding their way into model soldier and vehicle kits.

White Metal

Used for casting figures in scales 5mm to over 100mm, "white metal" is derived from the range of soft solders, which are tin/lead alloys with, for figure casting, antimony (in various proportions) added. Small traces of bismuth, copper and zinc can also be found in tin/lead alloys.

The more tin in an alloy means a better flow and superior definition to alloys with more lead content (which is used simply for bulk), but more tin means more expense and usually higher melting temperatures.

Pewter can be used and is lead free and rich in tin, but expensive. It moulds well, melting around 245°C, and produces highly detailed castings. Some model figures are cast — as limited runs — in pewter.

Back to white metal, of which there are many different types. It is not unknown for figure manufacturers to use more than one alloy for the same figure kit — the body cast in one type and any weapons (for greater definition on small parts and better strength) in another.

White metals used for casting model soldiers melt, depending on type, in the range 180°C — 250°C. Any castings produced should always be carefully cleaned to remove deposits and, because they contain lead, appropriate precautions should be taken when handling, even if it's only the odd white metal figure you assemble and paint.

Brass & Nickel Silver etched parts
The use of brass and nickel silver parts in the manufacture of white metal figure kits has become more widespread. Minute brass parts such as

buckles are etched out of the solid sheet by a photo-chemical process where the original is artwork, drawn many times larger, then reduced and transferred to the metal. The metal is covered with a chemical resist agent over (exactly) the areas of the part and then the sheet is immersed in an acid solution where the parts are left as the surrounding area is cut away by the acid. This process is also known as chemical milling.

Metal, in sheet form, is available for modelling purposes in model shop displays under various brand names. Aluminium tube and brass rods, squares, tubes and different sections are all available for the scratch-builder and converter. A stockpile of useful parts can be built up if a few parts are purchased at each visit.

WOOD

Wood is not as widely used as it once was by military modellers, in conjunction with card or paper, for building miniature vehicles, or for carving master figures. Plastic sheet and two-part epoxy fillers have replaced wood and card. Wood needs finishing before it can be painted — the grain needs filling otherwise paint just soaks in. However, wood should not be discounted as it is most useful for diorama use, particularly for buildings or interiors in boxed dioramas.

Balsa Wood Most people will be familiar with this lightweight soft wood, which is easy to carve with a sharp knife. A fine tooth razor saw is best for cutting balsa, especially thicker pieces. Balsa can be glued with Balsa Cement (cellulose) or PVA and similar water-based adhesives. Balsa can be sanded very easily but it needs sealing before painting.

Jelutong A light hardwood with an even texture and extremely close grain, jelutong carves beautifully and is a superb modelling medium. It will glue with most adhesives, but does not need as much grain sealing as balsa. Jelutong is not widely available and is expensive compared to other types.

Obeche Heavier than balsa, but still soft with a closer grain and even texture, obeche is very easily carved and sanded, and a cheaper but stronger alternative to balsa. However, sheet obeche can split very easily while being worked.

Spruce A stronger wood than obeche, spruce is a close-grained softwood which, because of its very straight grain, carves well. Spruce is flexible and in the solid can be used for complex carvings or producing master parts for mould-making, such as cast armour tank turrets.

Wood must be finished before painting. This can be done using a commercially produced grain-filler, but usually a couple of coats of varnish lightly sanded will suffice on small parts. Do not attempt to achieve saturation, but simply seal the grain. Try carving and experimenting with wood for small parts, for example a wooden crate in miniature can look realistic in natural wood rather than plastic.

Many older modellers began their hobby using wood and cardboard and although such materials have been superseded they should not be ignored.

Cardboard and paper While modelling in card is a separate hobby in itself, card and paper can be used in diorama work. For instance, paper, crumpled to "break" the texture, can be rolled to represent tarpaulins and then coated with diluted PVA glue.

Papers — especially tissue — are good for masking models during spraying or painting. Cards and thicker boards make good concrete slabs for base work. Cut up and positioned to the current pattern they can also be peeled to produce varying thicknesses. Always use a very sharp knife

Space-age technology applied to cyanocrylate adhesives from Pacer Tech of the United States. Each is formulated for specific tasks. The 'Zip Kicker' is an accelerator for cyano type glues.

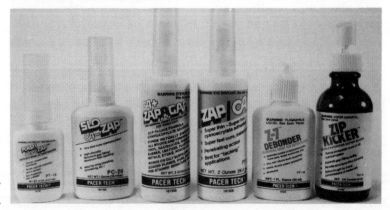

or scalpel, with a steel straight-edge, and cut on a purpose-built cutting mat or glass plate.

Most glues work on paper and card, from dry type glue sticks to PVA types. Both can be "sized" with varnishes to produce a smooth surface for paint. Shellac varnish used to be used for this purpose but varnishes of the polyurethane types work just as well.

Although cardboard has fallen behind the more convenient medium of polystyrene sheet it should be considered for many tasks where the latter can be a little too "rigid".

ADHESIVES
The terms "adhesive" and "glue" describe the same thing. There is no real difference but modellers should know the difference between the various types of adhesive especially when using dissimilar materials. What follows is a listing with a description of the more commonly encountered types.

Cyanoacrylates Also known as "superglues", cyano types have extremely fast setting times and will bond virtually any substances, with few exceptions, though unfortunately one is polythene. There are different types of these glues available now — some with gap-filling properties, quick setting, and slower setting thin types. Accelerators are available as sprays which cure them almost instantaneously on application.

Cyanoacrylate will bond skin, so extreme care should be exercised in its use. It can be thinned with most ladies' nail varnish removers, should any bonding occur which cannot be separated. Acetone-based nail varnish remover is also good for cleaning the tube nozzles which can easily clog to the cap, thus rendering the tube useless after using it only a few times.

Polystyrene cements Available in two basic forms, in a tube or "liquid" in a bottle for brush application, the adhesive is polystyrene dissolved in solvents. The tube cement can be quite powerful if used excessively, and can melt small parts to distort them. The cements work by dissolving both joining surfaces. Used correctly, the joint should be very strong.

Liquid cement is much thinner, volatile, yet easy to apply with a small brush. Although it works the same as tube glue

Liquid polystyrene cement secured in a Plasticine-filled coffee jar lid to stop the bottle being knocked over. The 'downgraded' paint brush is used for application.

its action is not as severe and it "runs" much better during application. Polystyrene cements can be non-flammable, but solvent vapours from any adhesives should be treated with caution.

Balsa cement Not strictly a cement, balsa glue adheres to porous surfaces such as balsa and most woods and other porous surfaces. It will not stick plastic. As far as military modelling is concerned, PVA glues will do the same job and they are cleaner and easier to use.

ABS Acrylobutyl Styrene plastic needs its own formula adhesive. Remember most plastics are joined by capillary actions of an adhesive made from particles of the plastic and other additives dissolved in a solvent. ABS "cement" is no different and it will also bond other plastics, especially polystyrene, though polystyrene cement will not bond ABS plastic with any degree of success.

Most ABS cements are supplied as liquids for brush

Liquid cements. Super Weld is DBI's glue for ABS, acrylic, lucite, etc., Liquid Poly for hard polystyrene, Tamiya's own brand and Faller's Expert which is applied via a long 'hypodermic' type tube.

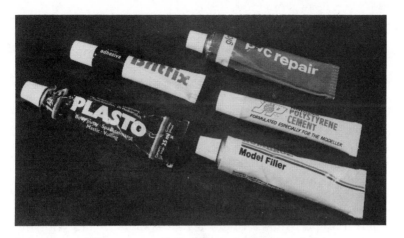

Tube glues and fillers are usually the first types tried by modellers.

application and often under trade names such as 'Micro Weld' (from "Plastruct").

Acrylic cement The military modeller will not have much demand for acrylic cements which are specifically designed for bonding acrylics, or Perspex as it is more commonly known. Acrylic cement contains the basic material — acrylic — dissolved in dichloromethane. Once opened the cement has a limited shelf life. It is a more virulent substance than polystyrene and is usually only available from specialist suppliers in quantities far in excess of the modeller's normal requirements.

PVA based products – adhesive, Rowney's Cryla Gloss and Acrylic gel medium. All are very useful for, for instance, representing water in dioramas, because they dry out to a clear state.

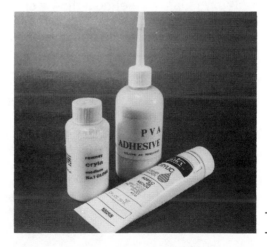

PVA Polyvinyl Acetate was designed as a general woodworking glue but it will bond most materials, porous or non-porous, rigid or flexible. It produces a film between the joining surfaces which is quite strong when set. However, PVA is water soluble, which can be a disadvantage but, as far as the military modeller is concerned, this feature can be used to advantage. Diluted PVA can be used to coat polythene figures and in ground work for scenics.

PVA dries transparent, although it is white when applied. It will soften after setting if soaked in water. Experiment with the glue whenever possible. It is probably the best adhesive for expanded polystyrene.

Epoxy Two-part glues where a hardener is mixed with the adhesive have been around for a long time. Before cyano glues became widely available, epoxies were the modeller's number one choice for sticking white metal figures together. They produce, if mixed and applied correctly, a virtually unbreakable joint.

The two-part glue must be mixed thoroughly and applied to both surfaces. There are many different setting times available, from about five minutes to curing times of over 24 hours. Joints should be supported and clamped while the glue fully sets and cures correctly. The resulting joints will be impervious to water and oil based paints, and also will have filled any gaps adequately, so lessening any "soak through" of covering materials, very important on, say, the arm joints on a white metal figure.

Epoxy glues are thermosetting resin types and their short "pot life" (i.e. the time the glue starts to set or "go off") after mixing can be accelerated by heat application. The addition of a hardener at room temperature starts the process, which is irreversible once mixing takes place. Epoxy has good electrical insulation properties and can also be moulded into small parts by the use of one-piece open moulds.

Contact adhesives General purpose contact glues are extremely useful and there are many different types which all work on the same principle — coat both surfaces with adhesive and allow them to become "tacky", then press together. Such adhesives produce firm bonds and come ready-mixed in a tube.

Warning

Adhesives should always be treated with caution. Do not breathe in any fumes given off or allow constant exposure or contact on the skin because many contain irritants. Do not sniff vapours as this could cause respiratory and brain damage.

	Polystyrene	Expanded Polystyrene	Polyester Resin	Polyurethane Resin	ABS Plastic	Acrylic (Perspex)	Balsa, Soft & Hard Woods	Card & Paper	White Metal
White Metal	C/G	B	C/G	C/G	C/G	C/G	G	C/G	C/G
Card & Paper	B/GH	B	G	G/H	C/G	C/G	BF/GH	BC/GH	
Balsa, Soft & Hard Woods	B/GH	B	G	G	G	G	BF/GH		
Acrylic (Perspex)	E	B	C/G	CE/G	CE/G	E			
ABS Plastic	D	B	C/G	CD/EG	D				
Polyurethane Resin	A	B	C/G	A					
Polyester Resin	CE/G	B	C/G						
Expanded Polystyrene	B	B							
Polystyrene	A								

A. Polystyrene cement
B. PVA cement
C. Cyanoacrylates ('Super Glues')
D. ABS cement
E. Acrylic cement
F. Balsa cement
G. Epoxy glues
H. Contact adhesives

Use this simple table as a guide to which adhesives will bond dissimilar materials. It is a 'guide' only and it will be found that cyanoacrylates, for example, will bond most of those materials listed, although it has not been listed for the majority. Cyanoacrylates do not normally work well on porous material, however, though constant applications will build up a 'seal' until bonding is made possible via saturation of the material's fibres.

Used carefully, and for tasks for which they were intended, adhesives are a boon. Abused they can be, at worst, killers. Keep them away from children, and locked away at all times when not in use. Always use adhesives, whatever their type, in a well-ventilated area, avoid eye and skin contact and always follow the manufacturers' instructions carefully.

PAINTS
Water soluble paints
Water colours, available in tubes and pans (blocks), are water soluble bound with gum arabic, and are only really good for absorbent papers. They are applied in transparent washes, are weak in colour and dry to a matt finish.

Gouache — or 'designer's colours' — are supplied in tubes but lack the luminosity and transparency of water colours. The paints dry to a matt finish and lighten as they dry out. They can be used carefully over a matt white oil enamel undercoat on figures but they will not stand handling.

Poster paint comes in tube, pot and powder form and is opaque when applied. Like gouache and water colour, poster colour is thinned with water. It can be used on figures suitably undercoated with white enamel. Casein added to water soluble paints, combined with a finely ground pigment, is marketed as 'Plaka' by the Pelikan Company of West Germany. 'Plaka' dries perfectly matt and is a popular choice for some figure painters. However, it must be worked very quickly because of its quick drying rate. Being finely pigmented, 'Plaka' sprays through the airbrush very easily once thinned and strained before use.

Acrylics have become very popular in modelling circles in recent years. Although they can be thinned with water their solvent base is ethyl alcohol and they come in tubes or pots, the latter being specifically designed for modellers. Intensity of colour and opacity are very good and by using additives the finish can be controlled through from matt to full gloss.

Once hard, acrylics are difficult to shift and so brushes and utensils must be cleaned with water immediately after use. Thinner for the solvent will break down any protective shell. Acrylics spray through the airbrush very easily, but it is recommended that solvent should be used for any final "blowing through" after a spraying session.

Emulsion paints are similar in consistency to acrylics. Though intended for household use, they have good modelling properties and can be used for scenic work. Crown Paints "Matchpots" while intended for DIY decorators to experiment with provide a good source for the military modeller. While all shades are not suitable they can be mixed and adapted with a little imagination. Also, like acrylic, they cover expanded polystyrene very well.

Oil Based Paints

Enamels are the best-known modellers' paints and are available in tins, bottles and aerosol cans. The thinner is turpentine or white spirit. Colour availability is extensive and shades produced specifically for military modellers are many. There are many theories governing how enamels should be applied and experimentation is advised. Use with airbrushes presents no problems so long as the paint is stirred then thinned and strained correctly. Humbrol market specially thinned enamels for the airbrush in quite a sizeable range of colours. Metallic enamels are quite easy to use but, unless sprayed on, can leave brush marks over large areas. Enamels are available in matt, semi-matt, or "eggshell" and gloss.

Oils are a favoured medium for figure painting. They come in tubes and are designed for picture painting. However, adapted by modellers they are most popular for painting figures on a flat enamel undercoat. Being totally intermixable they can be blended and worked for long periods before even beginning to dry out. Some can, in time, fade or yellow, so it's best to learn of their capabilities before use. Most dry to a slight sheen.

For figure painting, "Artists' quality" must be used. Any lesser qualities do not have such finely ground pigments and can be too coarse for use.

Oil paints are thinned with turpentine or linseed oil, though use of the latter is discouraged for painting miniature figurines as its addition produces too much oil and the colours take longer to dry out and the matt effect ideally required is somewhat lessened.

Alkyd colours such as those produced by Winsor and Newton are, like oils, pure pigments but ground in alkyd resin. They can be treated with the same materials and thinned with turpentine. Drying time is much shorter than oil paints but petroleum distillate will retard the drying time of alkyd colours. Alkyd resins are synthetics derived from alcohols and acids.

Cellulose Based Paints Cellulose paints will melt some plastics — especially polystyrene — and so they have not retained their popularity with military modellers, despite their suitability to painting white metal.

Available in tins, bottles and aerosols, cellulose is best applied over a self-etch primer on metals after they have been "degreased". ABS plastic will take cellulose, although polystyrene can "melt". However, if sprayed on in very thin coats, polystyrene can be covered. But why bother when enamels are less trouble?

Preparation and priming ready for painting
All materials should be prepared before the first brush is dipped into the paint, or the airbrush charged. Plastics, depending on the paint used, usually need a primer, as do woods and metals.

Plastic All plastics should first be washed in warm water and mild detergent. Injection-moulded plastic kit parts can carry remnants of mould release agents, which, although invisible to the naked eye, will impair paint adhesion. After assembly and filling, the completed model should be washed and allowed to dry naturally. Do not touch the surface with your fingers otherwise grease deposits will be transferred to the surface.

If using oil paints on a plastic figure, first prime the surface with matt enamel and use white or a shade complementary to the top colour to provide a "tooth" for the oil paint. With enamels or acrylics, it is unnecessary to prime the surface.

Polythene figures, after washing, should be primed with thin coats of diluted PVA glue which will dry to a hard shell and thus accept most paints. If using oils undercoat with matt enamel.

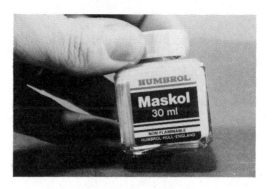

Masking fluid is, perhaps, the most under-used medium available to the modeller. Applied by brush it dries to a rubber skin and can be removed after painting is complete. It does not stain the surface to which it is applied.

Expanded polystyrene can be primed with thin coats of acrylic paints lightly sanded between each coat until the surface is sealed. The final coating of acrylic will form a plastic shell enabling even enamels which would otherwise melt expanded polystyrene to be safely applied.

Metal Any fluxes used for soldering should be removed with solvents and the figure or parts washed in warm soapy water. Similar treatment should be given to assemblies that have been glued. Scrub clean with toothbrush, then buff up, if possible, with a fine wire brush in a miniature power tool, then wash again ready for priming.

Metal must be primed to prevent later oxidisation. Self-etch cellulose primers or polyurethane varnishes are ideal. Finish by priming with matt enamel as a key for painting.

Wood Wood must have its grain sealed and the surface sanded before paint will form a fine smooth surface and not soak into it. Wood fillers are available which seal the grain with more than one coat, sanding between each. When smooth, prime with an undercoat before brushing or spraying the finishing coats. Multiple coats of polyurethane varnish can be used as a grain filler on most woods.

Card and paper Cardboard is easily sealed with varnish. Shellac used to be the one for the job, but polyurethane varnish is better. After coating, sand and then prime for painting. Paper can be soaked in diluted PVA glue and allowed to dry where it will set with a plastic coating which will readily accept paint. This is good for making tarpaulins and bed rolls out of paper for AFV models.

Fillers

Most kits and figurines usually require some sort of gap filler, necessitated by mould shrinkage or badly designed parts. All gaps must be filled before painting.

Plastic fillers Available in tubes, these fillers "attack" polystyrene surfaces and, if not used with care, can ruin a model's surface. They should be applied sparingly and in stages. Some can shrink during curing.

Plastic Padding (used for car repairs) is useful for filling large gaps and can be used for filling balsa wood parts for a smooth finish, such as on cast parts on model AFVs.

Epoxy fillers, the most popular in the UK being Milliput, are now indispensible. Masters for figurines are made in Milliput because once hardened it can be carved, drilled, sanded and shaped with engraving tools.

Epoxy fillers are two-part compounds, filler and hardener, which when mixed form a putty-like dough which will eventually harden. The cure rate can be accelerated with heat and the surface smoothed before curing with water or moistened tools.

Polyfilla and Tetrion Made for DIY home repairs and decorating, Polyfilla, especially the fine surface type, has many applications. Also known as 'spackling paste' it sticks to plastic well and to a lesser degree to white metal. It is most useful for basework on single figure displays or vignettes.

Milliput, the epoxy two part filler, has been used and praised by modellers for some years now. Two types are shown here, standard and silver grey. A white variety is also available.

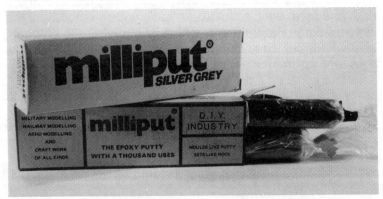

Diluted it can be used for "rendering" the walls of model buildings. It can be coloured with powder paint pigments before application.

Tetrion is a harder plaster very good for representing rough stonework on model buildings. It and Polyfilla can be used as wood grain sealers.

Low melt solders Solder has a gap-filling property and, once the art of soldering is mastered for figures and vehicles, all joints can be filled during construction or, if preferred, at a later stage.

Brushes

Brushes are an essential part of the military modeller's kit. Only the best sables should be purchased for figure painting because cheaper types, whatever their attraction, will not give the required result.

Red Kolinsky Sables are expensive, but probably the best. Experimentation will show which suits you best; some prefer smaller brushes with short hairs, while others go for longer bristles with a fine point. Examine the brushes before you buy.

Always keep your brushes scrupulously clean. After thorough cleaning with the appropriate solvent, wash them in warm soapy water and then "reform" the bristles and store upright in a pot with the bristles protected with a tube. Try not to mix your brushes, and if possible, use one set for oil, another for acrylic, and so on. This way, brush life will be prolonged.

Aerosol Sprays As an alternative to brush painting, aerosols are suitable for covering large areas and are useful for undercoating, especially on model figurines and vehicles where thin coats are possible, thus not obscuring any fine detail. Paint will deteriorate in aerosols and the can must be shaken throughly for at least two minutes before spraying. After use invert the can and spray to clear the nozzle. If possible, use an aerosol entirely in one spraying and always use them in a well-ventilated area.

Airbrushes An airbrush finish, correctly applied, is far superior to one made with a brush. However, a good airbrush is not cheap and neither is the compressor that powers it. Aerosol

Badger single-action airbrush and accessories. This airbrush can be supplied by either glass jar or metal cup. It is a 'middle of the road' model and once mastered, the Badger 200-6 produces excellent finishes.

cans are available to power airbrushes, but this is an expensive exercise. Airbrushing is a technique in itself and beyond the scope of this book. If possible, watch an airbrush in use, or ask for a demonstration of the equipment and have a try yourself.

4 MINIATURE FIGURINES

Collectors of miniature figurines fall, generally, into two groups, those who assemble and paint figures and those who convert and scratchbuild — painters and modellers.

The high standard of commercial figurines today leaves very little for the collector to do, except assemble, prime and paint. However, the figure modeller will still convert, adapt and scratchbuild from 'spares' or completely from scratch, doing all the sculpture from the armature upwards.

In figure competitions there are often different categories or classes to differentiate between painted-only figures and scratchbuild or conversions. Often the reverse is the case and when a scratchbuilt figure competes against a painted commercial figure the judge takes into account the 'work done' on the model and not just that it's 'a good paint job!'

The fully round figure is now universally popular, whatever the scale. The flat figure, formerly the most commonly encountered, is now not as popular, although flats are still available in large numbers, especially from Germany and they still command a following. Many modellers will paint flat figures as well as fully round ones.

FLAT FIGURINES

The flat figure is a two-dimensional miniature and the most popular scale is for 30mm tall figures although larger ones are available. Traditionally the figures are cast in slate moulds which are two-piece assemblies and have both halves hand-engraved by the sculptor. Being two-dimensional the figure shows both front and back detail. This is not always finished on both sides at the painting stage if the figure is to be displayed in a frame with only one side showing — a common form of display.

Flats of Roman Legionaries by Droste of West Germany. These are 30mm scale.

If both sides are visible then, of course, both should be painted. Painting flats is akin to painting a picture and skill is needed to make a one-dimensional object appear round, with relief. Also, the work is precise because of the scale when the figures are only 30mm high. A flats painter must, indeed, be skilled in the use of the brush and know the capabilities of his paints backwards. Flats are usually displayed 'flat' in a display frame on a single colour background. They can also be utilised in a diorama form on an open base, or in a boxed diorama with artificial lighting. Whatever the display feature, flats are best viewed directly onto the side, at perfect right-angles, otherwise the illusion is lost.

Although flats are mostly cast in white metal, injection moulded plastic (polystyrene) ones were produced in France some years ago. Some of these were semi-round too, and not perfectly 'flat'.

Flats have also been cast in metal in centrifugal casting machines, a far cry from the traditional slate moulds originally used.

Little can be done, nor, perhaps, should be, in converting flats, as they are intended purely as "painters' figures." Traditionally they are painted with artists' oils to make possible the subtle blending needed to create the illusion in highlight and shade.

Colours must be kept bright and precise on flat figures. It's no use allowing them to become muddy in appearance, otherwise the precise colour values and effects needed will be destroyed.

For the modeller flats are not really expensive. Considering the amount of time needed to paint one, and the enjoyment gained as entertainment value, they are

A war elephant flat, 30mm scale, painted by Jim Woodley. Photos show one side painted and the other left in bare metal and intended for a 'frame' type display.

Unusual semi-round figures, injection moulded in plastic, from France.

unbeatable. However, make no mistake about it, figure painting should be regarded as a pastime and fun, and never the chore that some people seem to make it.

After undercoating with either matt white enamel or cellulose car spray primer, you simply mount the figure on a piece of card, with a split cut in it to take the figure's base, and paint away after the priming coat has thoroughly dried out. If you don't like the first attempt, or the progress at any stage, simply wipe the oils off and start again. This is one of the major advantages of the oil medium in figure painting when compared to other types of paints.

ROUND FIGURES

Round figures, in any scale, moulded in white metal or plastic, are extremely popular with military modellers. Regarded by many as a three-dimensional art form, a well-painted figure is a joy to behold and does invite attention and interest from anyone who appreciates such artistry. They can also command a high price from collectors, but more often it's the casual observer who is fascinated, and who is so taken with the painted miniature that another military modeller is born. A lot of people look, admire and then want to have a go themselves. It's a well-known fact that most military modellers began their hobby by admiring the work of others. Round figures in the main are usually extremely well-made and detailed. Cast in plastic, resin, or most commonly, in white metal, there is a large selection to choose from in scales ranging from 30mm to around 100mm high, of which 54mm, 75mm and 90mm are the most popular sizes, or scales.

Figure designer at work. Major Bob Rowe of Ensign Miniatures working on a master 54mm figure. Note the magnifier used for fine work. Major Rowe works exclusively in metal.

In 54mm scale, the traditional size, modellers are fortunate enough to have plenty of separate parts available from which to *make* figures, not just assemble and paint kits.

Plastic figures became widely available in the 1950s and were initially moulded in polythene (more correctly *polyethylene).* They were intended as toys, and are still regarded as such — perhaps wrongly — by some modellers.

Different scales from different manufacturers. These are, from the left, nominal scales quoted, 1:35, 1:32 (54mm), 75mm, 80mm and 90mm.

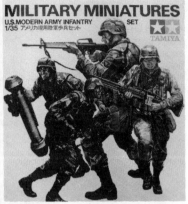

MILITARY MINIATURES

U.S.MODERN ARMY INFANTRY SET
1/35 アメリカ現用陸軍歩兵セット

TAMIYA

Plastic figures to 1:35 scale
designed by Tamiya to complement
their 1:35 scale modern armoured
fighting vehicles to enable dioramas
to be built.

Left, polythene 1:72 scale figures as
produced for the mass market.
These are British Victorian period
infantry produced by ESCI of Italy.

The moulded detail on these figures was very good and superior to anything on the market at that time. Many modellers would have preferred the figures to be moulded in the more rigid polystyrene but it was to be some years before Historex of France and Airfix in the UK mass-produced figure kits in this type of plastic, causing an instant 'boom' in the hobby. Some white metal figures were also being produced and some modellers even put metal heads on plastic bodies — the pure 'figure painters' may have thought it sacrilege but some beautiful models were produced in this way.

Plastic figures are moulded in expensive multi-unit steel moulds fed with molten plastic under great pressure, enabling mass production, whereas white metal figures, as far as the model figure market is concerned, are cast in hardened vulcanised rubber moulds on a centrifugal casting machine. Both systems need a master figure to begin with — only the form of casting and the material used are different. Plastic master figures are usually sculpted to a much larger scale than the finished product and are pantographed down to scale and cut into the steel mould; metal figures are produced from same-size masters normally, the process being not entirely different from injection moulding but slightly less technical as far as machine tools are concerned.

Painting fully rounded figures is really a matter of taste — and very personal in principle. Many words have been exchanged over what is the best paint, how to apply it, should additives be used, and so on. In the end, experimentation on the modeller's part is the key. By all means copy styles at first, but adapt and, where possible, improve on your first efforts. Practice *does* make perfect as far as painting military miniatures is concerned.

PLASTIC FIGURES

Plastic figures are preferable to many modellers as they are easier and more convenient to work than white metal. Plastic sticks easily — except polythene types — and can be cut, filed and bent to different configurations.

At the time of writing the largest range of plastic figures is that produced by the French company Historex. The future of the Airfix range of 'Multipose' types appears currently to be less certain. However, the Airfix polythene figures are widely available. These ranges are nominally described as 54mm, but the Historex range is 1:30 scale and Airfix 1:32 scale. The theory has been put forward that one (Historex) type was measured from the ground to eye level and the other to the top of the head! People are different in shape and thus it is much easier to work things out as a ratio.

Polythene figures

Polythene figures can be painted but first they must be washed in warm water and detergent (washing up liquid is good for this) to remove any surface grease and mould release agents, and then cleaned up by removing the mould separation marks which will be found going right round the figure. These cannot be filed nor sanded away; polythene is far too 'oily' in texture for this. A really sharp blade (such as a brand new scalpel blade) is necessary to pare away carefully any ridges and flash. Straight cuts should be made, not a scraping action, but be careful not to cut into the plastic because it cannot be filled with putty. The surface must be treated to accept and retain the paint. Polythene will not take paint directly onto its surface with any permanence, but if the figure is treated with water-diluted PVA glue, a greater degree of success is possible.

Paint the diluted PVA glue (Unibond is an old favourite for this process) over the figure. Two thin coats are better than one thick coat and allow it to dry out into a hard thin shell which shrinks over the figure enabling undercoating and painting along conventional lines to be carried out.

Conversion of polythene figures does present problems. As mentioned earlier, polythene is one of the groups of 'unstickable' plastics and thus any arms or body halves must be pinned for strength before coating with diluted PVA glue.

Recent experiments have shown that cyanoacrylate glues may 'hold' polythene, though not, it appears, with any permanence. Any texturing, such as hair, can be worked with a pyrogravure, though care must be taken because mistakes are not easily rectified.

Polystyrene figures

Hard polystyrene figures are easy to assemble, detail, prime and paint. Assembly with a polystyrene cement could not be easier and polystyrene does not have any of the minus points of its stablemate polythene.

A Historex plastic kit for a personality figure. Marshal Ney, 1769-1815. Note the many small parts on their runners and the horse halves.

After washing all parts in warm water and mild detergent to remove the usual surface deposits, any mould part lines can be removed with knife and file. When assembling a figure from a kit, a 'dry run' to ensure the fit of parts is recommended. Plastic of the polystyrene type does not require priming, but a coat of matt enamel is advised to give a 'tooth' to any paint used to finish and to show up discrepancies on the figure's surface. Do not use cellulose-based auto-primers on polystyrene: it sometimes works if the spray is misted onto the plastic but there can be a reaction and, at worst, the moulded detail on the surface may be completely destroyed. Enamels and acrylics can be painted onto polystyrene without an undercoat.

Polystyrene figures are good for converting and quite interesting types can be made up from spare parts such as bodies, legs, arms, heads, etc., to produce a figure not available as a kit. Of course, uniform distinctions will have to be added from modelling materials or adapted from the parts.

Further animation is possible by cutting arms and legs and repositioning them. Bodies can be twisted and heads turned, raised to look up or lowered to look down. Polystyrene can be worked with the pyrogravure; detail such as hair, fur trimming

Not all figures are military. These 18th century period civilians are from Phoenix Model Developments.

Conversions in plastic. These three figures are all made up from the same basic Airfix Multipose parts, cut and animated into different marching positions. Figure at right awaits head and arms and will be carrying a machine-gun over the right shoulder.

on uniforms, head-dress plumes, horses' manes and tails will benefit from careful modelling with this useful instrument. After modelling is completed, the figure should be, once again, washed in warm water and mild detergent solution before undercoating (if required) and painting.

Modelling in polystyrene, using spare parts from Historex and, when available, Airfix 'Multipose', limits the builder to 54mm (1:32 scale) or to 1:35 scale if Tamiya figures are used. Larger figures, 1:12 scale from Tamiya and Airfix can be adapted. Tamiya's racing driver and pit crew figures will be found to be somewhat short in stature but some excellent conversions have been made with them as they are reasonably priced and easy to work, being of hollow construction.

Very recently some highly-detailed figures moulded in polyurethane resin have been produced in Japan. This resin has the same working properties as polystyrene and although the figure range is limited to German WW2 types the detail on them is extra fine. Francois Verlinden is also about to release ranges of multi-pose type figures cast in polyurethane resin. Both manufacturers are working to a nominal working scale of 1:35, though the Verlinden types come out at around 1:33 scale!

For larger plastic figures, the Italian company ESCI produce a 1:9 scale German WW2 infantryman than can be

Multi part figures in white metal from Chota Sahib of Brighton. All are modern British army and the parts can be interchanged for various permutations.

converted into different configurations — an avenue definitely worth exploring for the modeller who fancies larger scale figures.

WHITE METAL FIGURES

'White Metal' figures are, usually, cast in hardened or vulcanised rubber moulds on centrifugal casting machines. The alloys used basically comprise lead, tin and bismuth, and are melted down in thick-walled melting pots, usually with some form of temperature control, and poured in a molten state into the spinning mould on the centrifuge. Depending upon the skill of the pattern and mould-makers, a high definition casting results, but it is this skill in both fields that separates a good figure from a bad one.

White metal figures can be even more detailed than their plastic counterparts. They are certainly heavier but they do cost more because of the very nature of their production and the materials used in their manufacture. However, for what you get they represent good value for money, and when painted up . . . well, that's another story.

A lot of modellers will shrink from converting a metal figure though they will 'leap into action' on a plastic one, wielding the modelling knife with infinite dexterity. However, converting metal figures is not really difficult — it just takes more time and a lot more care . . . especially when the cost is fresh in your memory as you reach for the coping saw.

This is the reason why so many similar metal figures are seen in competition, modellers preferring to paint rather than convert to be just that little bit different. Although there is on the surface nothing wrong with this concept, it does limit creativity to some degree. If you have any intention of entering competitions it would be well to bear this in mind.

White metal figures are normally very easy to assemble if the job is not rushed and every care is taken. Glues, such as epoxy resin and cyanoacrylate types, will do the job admirably but these figures can also be soldered together with the special low-melt solders that are available, using a temperature-controlled soldering iron.

White metal figures can range from a one-piece casting with only the base to add, to quite complicated kits where the military modeller has to assemble everything himself. The excellently-produced kits by master modeller Ray Lamb, in his Poste Militaire range, spring to mind, offering the modeller complexity and finesse of casting previously not thought possible. Imagine a complete horse harness in 90mm scale, for example!

The modeller should always first wash white metal figure castings in warm water and mild detergent, by totally immersing all the castings and then giving them a good scrub

Component parts of a 90mm white metal figure kit and wooden base.

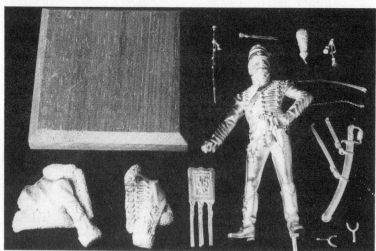

with an old tooth brush, ensuring it gets into every nook and cranny. This procedure is necessary, and more so than with plastic figures, to neutralise and remove any mould release agents still adhering to the castings. When all has been done, rinse and blot dry with soft paper tissue or allow to dry naturally. Try not to handle the figure too much until after assembly.

The next stage is to remove any flash and mould part lines. If the mould in which the figure was cast is good and the caster knows his business, then there should be no 'flash' on the castings at all. 'Flash' is caused by a badly-fitting mould where the metal flows from the cavity between the faces of the mould producing a 'membrane', for instance between a figure's legs.

The standards achieved in figure casting have virtually eliminated 'flash' completely but, if it is evident, remove it with a knife and files.

Mould parting lines, however, are virtually 'hair lines' on a good figure and they are the result of the contour of the joint lines of the two-piece mould where it follows the natural break, or part, line around the figure to eliminate any 'undercuts'. Undercuts, of course, would not allow the figure to be easily removed from the mould and are therefore eliminated by the mould maker by routing the mould part line in the most convenient position. More thought goes into

A single figure casting being polished up with a wire suede brush.

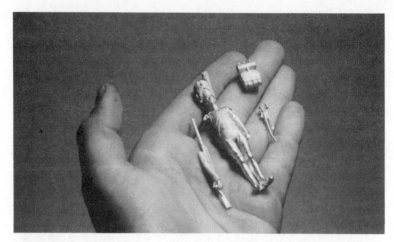

White metal 54mm figure kit of Chota Sahib's Imperial French Grenadier consists of four parts.

Trying the fit of parts in a 'dry run'.

mould making today, where once standards were less and it was common to find a mould part line centrally down a figure's face causing terrible distortion and also proving the very devil to remove without destroying much of the facial detail, the main attraction of any figure. Now these are made laterally, across the head and behind the ears. Also, where possible, heads are moulded separately for greater flexibility in production.

Mould hair lines can be scraped away with a knife and finished off with a needle file. Care must be taken to ensure

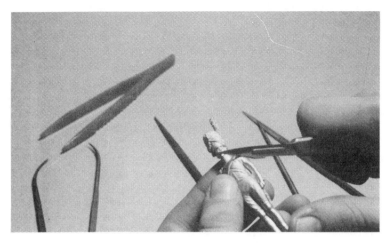

Removing mould part lines on the casting with a modelling knife.

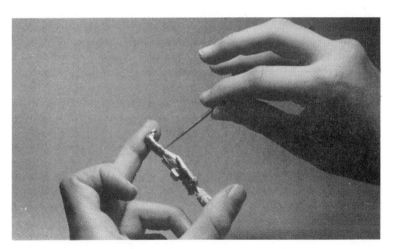

Fine 'Swiss' file in use cleaning up the castings.

that no detail is obscured during this operation and that any fine work incorporated by the pattern-maker is not obliterated by the careless application of simple hand tools.

When all parts have been cleaned up, assembly can begin. However, before reaching for the glue or soldering iron, it must be determined — especially with kits of many components — just how much will be obscured and inaccessible to the paint brush after final assembly. If any parts fit this category, and after a dry assembly run it will become clear which these are, they should be set aside and

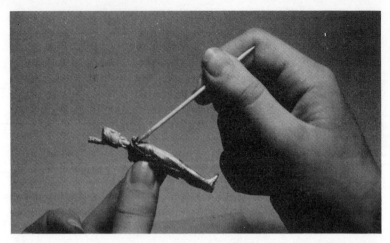

Applying epoxy glue with a wooden cocktail stick to fix the right arm in place.

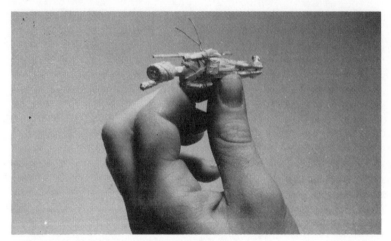

The arm wired for support until the glue cures.

primed and painted separately, later to be added to the main casting when all paint is dry, leaving only final 'touching in' with paint where the joints appear.

Glued assembly for white metal figures is by far the most popular method among modellers. Some modellers, however, do prefer soldered assembly and this will be discussed later as a guide to those versed in the practice of soldering in other spheres.

Epoxy resins are the most suitable adhesives for white metal figure kits. Two varieties are commercially available —

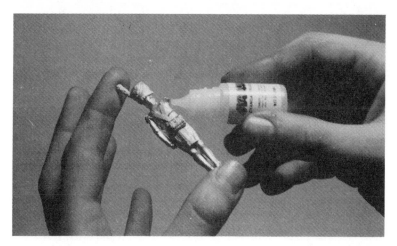

Cyanoacrylate glue being applied from its dispenser directly onto the joint as an alternative to epoxy.

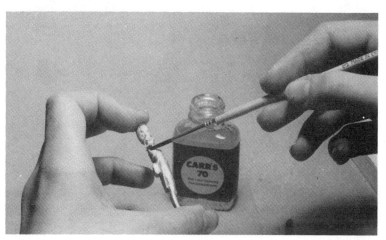

Soldering sequence commences by cleaning then applying flux to the joint.

the 'normal set' and a 'quick set' or 'five minute' epoxy. Whichever you choose, always read and follow very carefully the manufacturer's instructions for mixing the glue. Also, always ensure that bonding surfaces are scrupulously clean. Fine cross hatching with a knife blade does aid adhesion and should be done whenever possible, especially on flat butting surfaces.

A thin layer on both surfaces to be joined is made with a tiny spatula or a wooden cocktail stick; the latter can get into all areas, such as the locating holes for arm spigots. When

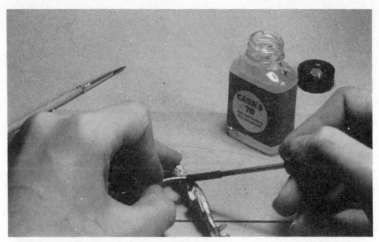

Joint is 'tinned' with Carr's 70 low-melt solder.

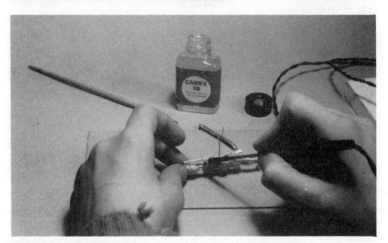

Parts wired together then 'sweated' with the soldering iron.

the pieces are brought together they should be supported, clamped or wired where possible — or both! Leave the glued parts until the adhesive cures thoroughly but ensure that any excess glue that may have oozed from the joints is wiped away. Its removal later may prove rather difficult.

Heat will accelerate the setting time of epoxy whereas cold slows it down somewhat. Do not, however, put white metal figures near direct heat sources such as cooker grills or place them in a domestic oven. While this *can* be done successfully, some modellers ignorant of the low melting point of white metal have reduced prized figures to pools of

The assembled figure mounted on a support ready for painting.

molten metal. If an oven is used, the figure should be suspended somehow or mounted on a block of wood, but not on a metal tray which will conduct all available heat and thus melt the figure.

If you're anxious to see a completed model, use the 'five minute' epoxy which does not give as much positioning time for tricky parts, but does 'go off' pretty fast when compared with the regular variety, whose pot time can be quite extended depending on conditions.

Epoxy bonds are virtually unpartable. Cyanoacrylates or 'super glues' (to give their popular euphemistic title, based on one of the first commercial trade names) will stick to white metal quite well. Their use is quick and clean and, above all, convenient. Although they possess initially as much strength as epoxy, experience has shown that rough handling can cause parts to drop off figures after some time and certainly larger joints can fail under pressure. The many modellers wielding tubes of 'super glue' at competitions, repairing 'broken' models, is testimony to this.

As with most products, improvements to cyano-type adhesives have been made. There are newer types on the market with gap-filling properties, which do work quite well and also accelerators in easy spray form which make these glues go off virtually immediately. They can, however, turn any exposed cyano glue white and powdery, and this deposit cannot be removed easily from any model's surfaces. Extra thin and cyanos especially formulated for plastic are also available. One day, perhaps, they'll have one for polythene, but it seems unlikely!

'Super glues' are extra-thin and can ooze out of joints and run down the model very easily if care is not taken, so apply them sparingly. Also, watch your fingers; skin can be bonded to the model figure very easily. Debonders are available that will neutralise the adhesive and ensure a 'clean' and painless parting where skin is concerned.

As an alternative to adhesives, soldering is not really difficult for figure construction. That said, however, many beginners would not agree and many would also not even attempt to solder a figure together at all. The only equipment needed is a temperature-controlled soldering iron, the low melt solder and the correct flux for the job.

There are, basically, two methods of joining parts together on white metal figures — direct application of the solder and soldering iron together on a fluxed joint and sweating the components together to produce a neat and automatically-filled joint. As with glue, all mating surfaces must be clean, but on white metal it helps if they are first burnished with a wire brush. This offers a superbly-shiny surface for excellent flux dispersion and adhesion.

The flux is all-important in soldering. The solder will not flow in the joints where flux is not present; it simply 'balls up'

Sunlec plastic modelmakers' clamp used to hold an arm in place while the epoxy glue sets. These clamps are tensioned with elastic bands and very useful.

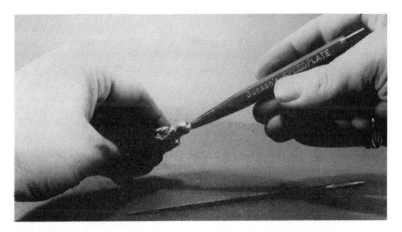

A fibreglass pencil in use to smooth and shine up white metal figure castings.

into globules and will not disperse correctly. Direct application of iron and solder to suitable joints works well if the flux has been applied sparingly. However, support of the parts is necessary because the solder takes a few seconds to solidify. Remember, iron and solder must be applied simultaneously to the fluxed joint for the best results.

Securing figures to white metal bases, as supplied with some figures, is very easily carried out by this method. By working from underneath the base the spigots on the bottom of the figure's feet can be 'invisibly' secured, allowing no solder to come between the soles of the figure's feet and the base.

Arms, heads and such extremities cannot normally be soldered directly, but they can be sweated into place. Clean and flux both jointing surfaces, then give each a thin skim or film of solder. Locate the part and support it — in the case of an arm, wire to the body and compress the joint with a wire

Figures designed to complement military vehicles. These are 1:35 scale white metal figures from Barton.

twist. Apply a clean soldering iron to the arm and observe the joint, watching for the solder to liquefy due to heat conduction and then transfer to the solder within the joint. The solder has a much lower melting point than the metal the figure is made from, so no damage will be done to the surface of the casting where the iron is applied.

If possible, apply more pressure to the joint as the solder melts; if compressed a little more, as the solder melts it will exude from the joint. When the joint is made, any excess solder around it can be removed with a quick wipe with the iron; but do not apply any flux on the joint and do clean the iron's bit with flux first.

After soldering is completed, wash the figure in warm soapy water, Washing up liquid is an excellent flux remover and all residues must be removed from the surface. Next check for any gaps or surface pitting which can be filled or 'stopped' with more solder, then give the figure a final wash.

Before priming give the figure the last 'once over' — you're bound to have missed something and it would be very difficult to correct when you're half way through painting the figure. If you have used glues, epoxy or cyano, check especially the arm, head and leg joints if the kit is multi-part.

Priming

Priming white metal figures before painting is necessary for the paint to adhere to the castings and it should be done carefully — always! It not only shows up any imperfections missed in the other preparatory stages but provides a good undercoat for any colours used. White metal, untreated, is a very poor medium on which to paint, especially if you wish to use oil paints.

Before priming, the castings should be spotless; don't hesitate to wash the figurine as much as possible as the paint will adhere all the better for it. But always ensure that you rinse thoroughly in cold clean running water straight from the tap. Some modellers don't even wash the casting once from taking it out of the box, gluing it together and then painting it, then wonder why the paint won't stick and in a short time wears off or even, in some cases, flakes away. There are, of course, those who will tell you that washing the castings is all baloney and that it is not necessary. The choice is yours.

Priming can be sprayed or brushed on. The former application is preferable because it ensures (if done correctly) that a fine coat is evenly distributed all over the figure. Brush application if done carefully, however, works well and should not be looked upon as inferior.

Choice of the primer colour is personal and one that will be adopted with experience. Clear varnish, matt white enamel or light grey enamel are all used, as are the basic colours — in enamels or acrylics — that the figure will, ultimately, be painted in. For a figure with a red tunic and blue trousers, for instance, matt red and blue enamels are painted on directly over the white metal. This ploy is used by some modellers who paint exclusively in oils.

If metallic enamels are to be used, undercoat black or dark blue for iron, yellow for brass and bronze and white or very light blue for silver. Again, experimentation is advised.

Matt white auto primer spray is an excellent undercoat and primer for white metal figures. It is cellulose based, but this does not matter on metal surfaces. Any paint can be applied over the top of it and it is durable, drying to a perfect matt finish with a very fine grain, favoured by some modellers as a

White metal figure kits from Poste Militaire, assembled and undercoated with white sprayed-on primer.

White metal figures from Cheshire Volunteer assembled and undercoated with Humbrol matt white, brush-applied, ready for painting.

good key for paints. Auto primer paints can be found in any shop dealing with motor spares, such as the national chain of Halfords stores.

Matt white enamel sprays are ideal too but, if the can is not shaken properly or for long enough to thoroughly mix the paint, a less-than-satisfactory result is definitely on the cards. Most aerosols include internal 'agitators' which should be rattled for a good five minutes or so before spraying. You simply do not know how long the can has been standing on the shelf before you bought it.

A point to remember when spraying with aerosols, or any spray equipment for that matter, is not to make one heavy application in one pass of the can. Several thin coats, 'misted' onto the model figure works far better than one heavy coat and gives a much more satisfactory finish. Remember, too, always spray in a well-ventilated area and, when finished, always cover the figure to stop dust particles settling on the drying surface. Keep the can at a respectable distance from the model figure too and if possible, wear a disposable mask during all spraying. Try blowing your nose after any prolonged spraying session to see what you've breathed in – you could be surprised!

Brush priming is probably the most common method used for undercoating miniature figurines and thinned white enamel is the most common undercoat used. As with spraying, apply thin coats, ensuring 'pockets' of dried paint do not form in the creases and other such areas on the figure. Use at least a No. 5 brush and do not overload the bristles with paint before use. Always allow primer coats to dry for at least 24 hours before painting otherwise you could find, if you're impatient to get going, that the paint you use could 'lift' the undercoat.

After you've primed a figure do not handle or finger its surface again. Make final checks for surface imperfections and, using a clean tissue to handle the figure, mount it on a handle so it can be manipulated during the painting stages. It must be secured so that it will not part company with the holder when held at various angles from the horizontal to the vertical. For smaller scale figures a piece of large-diameter wooden dowel, such as a piece cut from a broom handle, with a small square of wood screwed to one end, will suffice to mount the figure on. The figure can be secured to this with Blu Tack or self adhesive pads available in stationers.

However, anything over 54mm scale is not really suitable for this method, so for larger figures, where the mass of metal dictates a really secure mounting, alternative methods are needed. If the figure has a cast base in the kit, secure this by drilling a hole in it (don't worry – it can be filled later) and putting a woodscrew directly through it into a wooden handle. Do not position the screw hole so that the figure, or parts of it, will be over the screw or removal later on may be a problem. Also ensure that the holes in the base to take the spigots of the figure's feet do not foul the handle.

Where no cast metal base is supplied, or spigots are absent from the feet, holes must be drilled up into the feet and brass rod spigots or threaded bolts inserted and secured with glue or solder. These can then be inserted in pre-drilled holes in a block of wood or similar.

Drill the hole into the bottom of the feet, into the heels, and thus into the mass of metal constituting the leg, for a short way. This will give a more secure support and be less likely to come adrift during painting, which would be an absolute disaster.

Alternatively, a self tapping screw or bolt could be used to secure the figure to a plywood or thick plastic plate via the drilled hole. The plate could then, in turn, be secured to a handle ready for maximum support during painting.

Whatever the method used the figure must be absolutely

secure for painting. It's nigh on impossible to hold a figure by its extremities while you paint it. Besides, it defeats the object of cleanliness and the natural oils in the skin of the fingers will be transmitted to the model, thus destroying the smooth clean primer surface.

Take time over your preparations and don't rush them. The old saying of 'spoiling the job for a ha'porth of tar' certainly holds true here.

We have touched on converting metal figures, albeit briefly, and stated that it is a practice not many modellers, especially beginners, care for. A conversion can exist in many forms. Simple additions to a stock figure and a different paint job could be termed a conversion, and would certainly make it different from the stock castings made up and painted from the kit to the manufacturer's instructions. It is a challenge and fun, however, to cut and reposition arms and legs in a different posture, so altering the figure considerably. Also, interchanging of parts, even plastic and metal, works, so don't be afraid to mix your mediums at any stage of the game. All you have to do is ensure that everything is in proportion because one manufacturer's concept of a common scale may not match that of another.

Some one-piece castings cannot really be converted but characters can be changed by simply altering the position of

Assembled and undercoated white metal horse mounted on a wooden block ready for painting.

Constructors and painter's kit. Many different types of paint are shown ranging from enamels and acrylics (left), through painting mediums to oils on the right. A soldering iron and flux is at right. Centre is a glazed pottery palette – invaluable for mixing oil paints.

the head, which, in fact does cause considerable change of any figure's posture. Just compare the stock casting with one where the attitude of the head has been altered, and this becomes clear.

Major conversions are not easy for beginners, who may look upon any mistakes as very expensive, and these are something that should be worked up to, but if you can convert plastic figures with complete success, metal should not prove difficult at all.

A fine piercing saw is a necessity and a soldering iron does make life much easier than glue and a lot of filler. Make sure all cuts in white metal are made cleanly and that the work is always well-supported and securely clamped while you attend to it. It is something that requires practice and a logical step-by-step approach.

White metal figures can be 'carved' to a limited degree but it is much easier to remove metal – and replace it – with a soldering iron. Begin with simple conversions – such as interchanging parts, altering head, arm and leg positions – and graduate to completely different postures which should give you practice for scratchbuilding your own figures at some later date.

Find out which manufacturers have 'spares' in their ranges. This is no problem for plastic figure converters with the vast Historex range of spares, but Scale Link, Verlinden in

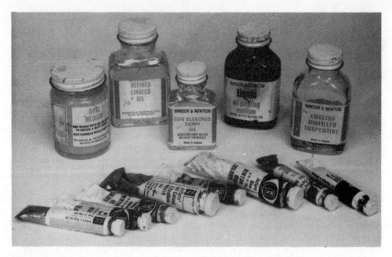

Oil paints in tubes and their mediums behind. Find out all you can about paint additives and experiment with them on scrap.

Belgium and Puchala in West Germany all produce heads for converters and scratchbuilders; bare heads and ones with various forms of head-dress are available and these ranges are definitely worth investigation.

Larger scale modellers are not so well catered for as the 54mm figure modeller but, with a lot of searching, various spares including firearms and swords can be found. Once you've mastered human conversions, try horses – in metal they're a whole new 'ball game' when compared to the plastic types.

PAINTING

Painting a figure cannot really be taught from a book, and again, practice and experimentation are needed. Guidelines can be given, but ultimately it is down to the individual modeller and his or her dexterity with the paint brush that counts in the end. However, some 'do's and don'ts' can be passed on.

If you know someone who can paint figures, the obvious course is to sit down with him – if he's willing of course – and be shown how to paint, step-by-step from square one. Joining a local modelling club with military modelling as an exclusive interest should produce such a 'guiding light'.

Copy other modellers' styles and how they do it. Use the same mixes of colour and slavishly copy them until you become competent and proficient in the art and no longer need any guidance. When you are competent and satisfied with your results then deviate from the pattern you've become accustomed to following and develop your own style. This you must do, otherwise you will simply be a clone of your instructor.

The face of a model figure is all-important. An excellently painted face can 'lift' an otherwise mediocre figure whereas a not so good face can make an excellent figure mediocre. Realism is transmitted from a lifelike miniature face whereas a carelessly painted face simply destroys any illusion of realism. Not everyone is good with the brush, however, and in the end it is only practice and yet more practice that brings rewards.

At first keep your colour mixes simple and do not opt for many of the published 'multi-colour mixes' to obtain a flesh colour. Remember also that your painting must represent the figure as a human would appear from a distance. Begin about 15 yards or so away with a friend as the 'model'. Ask him or her to approach and notice how the facial details alter from obscure to distinct as the subject nears you. Then try it with you holding a figure at arm's length and the subject approaching to match that height in your direct forward vision. What you see on the human subject should form a rough guide to what you're trying to achieve on the miniature

The mixing-in of mediums is easily done on a palette (on sale in artists' suppliers) with a wooden cocktail stick.

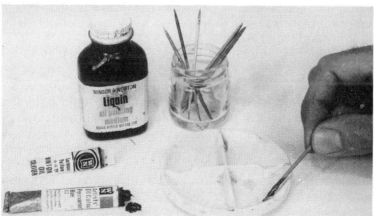

Sequence for painting a face, simply, in oils, shows an overall flesh tone applied to facial area.

Shadows (mix flesh tone and Burnt Umber) to eye-sockets, sides and under nose and lower lip, cleft of chin, around hair line and below jaw, into and behind ears.

figurine's face. So many people forget this and 'overpaint' the face to distraction. The heavy lines and shading produce something resembling the 'frog prince' which bears little resemblance to any human features. Turning what should be normal into something ugly is a trap that is easily fallen into. Although figures should be painted in similar style to an actor putting on make-up, they should not be overpainted to the point where they resemble a circus clown.

Eyes are very important. Never paint them black! Never paint eyeballs white and never show the eyeball completely, unless the figure is to be depicted in the act of some wide-eyed action pose. White for the eyeballs should have the merest touch of light blue – and eyeballs are brown, blue or green, or shades thereof, not black which is too severe a colour and will completely unbalance an otherwise correctly coloured face.

Painting in oils offers the added advantage of enabling unsuccessful attempts to be wiped away. With acrylics or enamels, wait until the paint dries then paint over it. Use a

This three-quarter view shows the same as the previous photo but from a different angle.

The hard edge of the shading is removed by blending into the flesh tone with a soft, dry brush.

brush well-suited to the task, one you're happy with, but not too big for faces. A 00 is a good one to start with when you're getting the feel of painting faces.

A basic flesh tint for European skins is mixed from yellow ochre and titanium white with a minute spot of red for fresh complexions. Darken this mixture with a brown tint such as Burnt Umber, in varying degrees, and use it as a shading tint. Highlight the mixture by adding more titanium white. Therefore your basic palette for flesh should have three pre-mixed shades before you begin. Follow the step-by-step photos to see how a 54mm figure's face (about 6mm high) is painted with oils.

Painting the uniform and clothing is next. Before you start you must ascertain from which direction the light comes and where the shadows and highlights will fall on the figure. As with flesh tones, darken or lighten the basic shades and apply shadows and highlights accordingly. Do not overdo this procedure and ensure that the colours blend and do not end in hard demarcation lines as they graduate from shadow to highlight. Once mastered the technique will become easier and virtually second nature. Brush out the paints thoroughly and do not overload the brush. The object is to

Using white in the flesh tone, highlights are added to cheekbones, bridge of nose and chin, then blended in.

Hair colour, including eyebrows and moustache, added. Here it's iron-grey highlighted with white.

spread the paint evenly and not to layer it on in thick coats. Blend with a dry brush on large areas such as clothing where light and shade must not be overpainted.

Different materials, such as fur, leather and metals, need different treatment. This is especially so if a convincing metal effect is to be achieved on plastic. As most clothing is matt in appearance, leather produces a contrast in that its surface is shiny. Fur also has highlights which it needs in the painting stage to emphasise depth.

'Metals' need an undercoat and finishing coat to seal the grainy surface they leave when dry. Enamel metallic paint should not be mixed in the tin, but the sediment scooped from the bottom, deposited on a palette and thinned to the required consistency with the solvent in which the paint is bound. It is then applied to the model, brushing out smoothly as you progress but trying also to avoid overpainting. Use two thin coats instead of one thick one.

A recent innovation in metallic colour is Humbrol's 'Metalcote', which contains metal particles. The paint is applied by brush – or preferably sprayed on by airbrush – then allowed to dry for about 30 minutes and buffed to a highly polished finish. Practice and experiment with these colours

has shown that, once again, two thin coats are better than one thick one. Unlike conventional metallic paints, and because they have metal particles added, 'Metalcote' colours should be stirred thoroughly. The sediment alone can be a little too thick and will not disperse correctly if thinned a little at a time to obtain correct consistency.

Extensively-converted Historex figures by Max Longhurst. Such excellent animation does a lot to 'destroy' the wooden appearance of the basic figures.

Breyer Stablemates are small scale models that can easily be adapted. The pyrogravure can be used on them too, the plastic being sufficiently soft.

As mentioned, ordinary metallics can dry to a grainy finish and benefit from a coat of polyurethane varnish – the clear variety – to produce a smooth finish more like a real metal surface. Do ensure that the paint has dried out completely before painting varnish over the top as varnish has a habit of lifting uncured paint very easily.

Where metallic lace is found on uniforms do not paint it in metal colours. Nothing looks worse, or more gaudy or unreal. Use paint, yellow ochre for gold, greyish blue for silver, highlighted and shaded to represent the lace. Experiment by adding a little gold powder which introduces minute highlights to the lace, but don't overdo it, and practise off the figure first.

Try all different types of paint for your figures and mix them together too. Experiment as much as possible to achieve different effects and try mixing enamels with oil paints, and also the different water-based types together. Try adding gesso powders and talcum powder to paint to see what effects you can achieve.

Horses are not easy to paint convincingly, especially when a beginner compares his first efforts with those of an experienced painter; it's enough to put anyone off . . .

A simple, yet very effective, method of obtaining a good finish on horses used to be demonstrated by Max Longhurst

A well-painted horse features in this vignette, a Historex conversion by Fred Whetnall which "tells a story".

some years ago, where he used a piece of sponge and oil paint to finish them. After assembly and priming the complete body was painted in oils of the darkest shade. Next a dry piece of plastic microcellular type sponge was lightly rubbed over the surface leaving the dark paint in all engraved detail and areas the sponge could not reach.

A highlighting colour on another piece of sponge was then applied with a dabbing motion over the area where the paint

General Montcalm, a Historex conversion by David Hunter to 54mm scale.

Different sizes of bases for models. The figure is 80mm scale.

was removed with the first wipe. This forms the basis of an overall finish and leaves only the eyes, hooves and any markings to be put on with the paint brush.

With horses always try to refer to a real subject whenever possible. Different colours and types of horse have different coloured muzzles, hooves and suchlike. If you have access to horses in a local stable where they can be seen without tack, take your camera and shoot some film of different colours to be used as painting references.

Different scale figures, 54mm left and 65mm right, mounted on the same base. Whereas only one 65mm figure is suited to the size, two 54mm figures fill the base nicely. Note the respective badges mounted on the base as an added decoration.

ENSIGN, LAMPLUGH'S REGIMENT OF FOOT

Simple scenic work on this base greatly enhances the figure's visual appeal.

Left, scratchbuilt figure about six inches tall by John Runnicles.

1ST SKINNER'S HORSE 1912

SCRATCHBUILDING FIGURES

Ultimately, many modellers will attempt to build a figure completely from scratch after using different commercial spare parts in complicated and advanced conversions.

Using Milliput for the first time also inspires many modellers. This useful medium, formed over an armature, is one of the most popular methods of producing a figure from scratch. It's also the easiest, especially for small scale figures.

The armature can be made up from wire; a loop for the head, single strands for the body, arms and legs, with perhaps some thickening in the trunk areas. The armature must be in correct human proportions otherwise something unhuman will result. Milliput mixed up in small quantities should be added in small balls or pellets until the body shape is built up.

The head deserves, and must get prime attention. It's not

Figures from the Musée de l'Armée, Paris, depicting French archers from the army of Charles VIII, c.1483. All the items of clothing and armour are from actual materials.

really worth continuing with the rest of the model unless you have a good representation of the human head to begin with. If you feel it is beyond your capabilities to sculpt a head, use one from a spares range or take one from a figure in the scale you're modelling in and adapt that. Expensive, but it meets the requirements! In 54mm scale, of course, a good selection is available.

For building up figures an alternative to the armature method is a 'dolly' which is the rough human shape, a sort of 'tubular skeleton'. From this can be cast, in RTV silicone rubber moulds, in white metal, as many 'dollies' as required. The metal castings will be thin enough to bend and animate before building up with Milliput to the required form. Once the ideal size is made and available as a casting, building up the rest in Milliput enables a collection of scratchbuilt figures to be built up fairly quickly.

5   MODELLING MILITARY VEHICLES

Modelling armoured fighting vehicles (AFVs) is a popular facet of the military modelling hobby. Once lavishly catered to by an obliging plastic kit industry, the supply of new releases has now slowed down to a trickle. Other areas have captured the attention of the toy industry. Yes, toy industry because, make no mistake about it, plastic kits of miniature military vehicles are a product of this industry. They have to be, for the capital needed for investment in injection moulded kits is considerable, and toymakers follow trends.

The manufacture of model vehicle kits is currently centred on two countries – Japan and Italy, with the French (with British encouragement) playing a back seat role. There is no British plastic kit industry at the time of writing although Humbrol are re-releasing some if not all of the Airfix range of plastic kits. Vehicle kits to 1:72 and 1:35 scales have been standardised by the Japanese and Italians, although there are also some larger and oddball scales. The British

A Tamiya 1:35 scale US M60 tank, a plastic kit built straight from the box, no details or paint applied, result, a plastic tank. The model lacks 'life' or purpose.

Tamiya's 1:35 scale Long Range Desert Group's Chevrolet truck kit, built as from the box, but painted and weathered. This is visually more pleasing and realistic.

company, Airfix, flirted with the idea of Military vehicle kits some years ago and decided to swim against the rest of the world by adopting the traditional model soldier scale of 1:32 for its models. This was 'supported' by Monogram, the famous United States company, whose output of 1:32 scale models was greater than Airfix's. Both companies produced excellent kits, although their output was nowhere near as prolific as the Japanese.

Tamiya's *Sdkfz 232* armoured car with simple additions of stowage, tarpaulin, water bottles, helmets, etc., and crew members is an improvement on the basic kit as supplied in the box.

Heller, the French plastic kit manufacturer, entered the field with some 1:35 scale models, mainly of, perhaps understandably, French vehicles. These were withdrawn from the market for some time but are once more available from Humbrol who have acquired the rights as well as those of the Airfix range.

Small scale vehicle modelling has always enjoyed a fairly large following in the United Kingdom where the scale of 1:76 has proved to be the most popular, despite the Japanese and Italian 'invasion' of 1:72 scale model vehicle kits. Based on the Airfix introduction of 1:76 scale plastic kits of AFVs in the

Tamiya's 1:35 scale Bradley Armoured Infantry Fighting Vehicle built straight from the box and airbrushed in the US Army's four colour camouflage scheme.

early 1960s, where modellers adapted and converted what was available, this aspect of the hobby has expanded and secured a devoted following. Airfix based the scale of 1:76 on the so-called model railway scale of 4mm = 1 foot or, as the kits were labelled, 00/H0, a confusion of scales because the British manufacturers had had to build the bodies of the locomotives to 4mm = 1 foot but adopted the continental track gauge of 16.5mm (4ft 8½in) based on 3.5mm = 1 foot or half 0 gauge (7mm = 1ft). Surprisingly a similar 'scale clash' was repeated by the Japanese Tamiya company with their early Sherman tanks where the lower hull and running gear scaled out nearer to 1:32 scale and the upperworks were near to 1:35 scale. The box said 1:35 scale, but modellers' rules said different. The 1:32 scale running gear did, however, come in useful for the many convertors and scratchbuilders in that scale!

Recently this mish-mash was perpetrated by the German manufacturer, Airmodel. Producing a new polyester resin kit of the Soviet T72 main battle tank, the running gear, hull and turret were all made to different scales, the kit being labelled 1:35 scale. The moral of all this is never take what's printed on the kit wrapper or box top as gospel . . . check it yourself.

It does seem, however, that 1:35 scale is the one modellers have settled for simply because there are more kits available to choose from. Monogram still have their 1:32 scale kits available and it remains to see what Humbrol do with the Airfix models. The United Kingdom does, however, remain a centre of 1:76 scale vehicle modelling and has a flourishing society, the Miniature Armoured Fighting Vehicle Association (MAFVA), for like-minded individuals to join.

Recently, smaller scale modellers have seen an upsurge in model production where polyester – and now polyurethane – resin models have become available in greater numbers in the very 'British' scale of 1:76. The wheel has turned full circle and it is hoped that larger scales will be produced in the near future. At the moment, some conversion parts are available in 1:35 scale and one complete kit, the Airmodel T72, has been released with more planned from this German manufacturer. The system has a drawback – cost!

Limited production in resin cannot match the cost per unit of injection moulded kits but modellers will pay for something they want – they always have – and thus the

Artillery models are popular too. This is Scale Link's 1:32 scale British 60pdr gun, built from a white metal kit.

Large scale kits can be fitted with radio control equipment, as in this Tamiya 1:16 scale West German *Gepard* anti-aircraft tank.

smaller manufacturers are receiving encouraging responses from their modelling clientele.

Injection Moulded Kits

Plastic injection moulded kits far outweigh models produced in any other medium. They are mass-produced and world-wide distribution facilities are available to the kit makers.

The amount of detail that can be incorporated into a plastic kit is phenomenal. Large scale patterns or master models are made which are then reduced to the required scale by a pantograph system which reproduces the parts in solid steel blocks which form the (normally) two halves of the injection mould. Molten plastic under pressure is forced into the mould to produce the parts to make up the plastic construction kit.

Resin Moulded Kits

Largely devoted to the smaller scales and smaller production figures, the resin kit manufacturers fill a considerable hole in the market and produce kits for AFV modellers who feel they cannot aspire to scratchbuilding.

The kits are produced from same-size masters, where the skills of the pattern maker decide on the amount of detail incorporated in the kit. Although not as sophisticated as their

Resin kit assembled of an Italian WW2 tank, a 1:76 scale P26/40. Note the amount of surface detail that can be incorporated in such models.

injection moulded counterparts, some resin kits are very highly-detailed.

Kits can be complex, but they usually consist of around six parts. In the case of a tank this would be the hull, two track units (moulded 'solid' with the wheels, sprockets, etc., in situ) the turret and gun. There may also be some smaller fittings such as exhaust silencer, anti-aircraft machine-gun or even a commander figure.

Polyurethane plastic resin is beginning to supersede its less-manageable stablemate, polyester. The former gives a much better definition in the mould and is easier to mix and pour, having a finer consistency, and it is less prone to the

Don't disregard 1:87 scale military vehicles which come assembled from many finely moulded plastic parts as this Roco German army truck.

masses of air bubbles that seem to dog polyester resins during casting.

Polyurethane is not as brittle as polyester and can be assembled with ordinary plastic glues. It is far superior in many ways, not least in its ability to form finely detailed parts which would be impossible to mould with polyester.

Resin kit manufacture is bound to break into 1:35 scale military vehicle circles. Conversion parts for 1:35 scale modellers are now available, so it appears that it is only a matter of time before the military vehicle modeller will once again have a wider choice of kits.

Vacu-formed Plastic Kits

Really available from only one major producer, Airmodel of West Germany, vacu-formed kits have not really been popular, perhaps because they need so much work doing to them to bring them up to acceptable standards. Once the assembly sequence is seen many modellers would rather scratchbuild anyway. Vacu-formed models are not easy to build and beginners are advised to stay away from the temptation of a comprehensive availability list until they are quite competent at assembling and converting injection moulded plastic kits.

Metal Kits

One or two-piece small-scale white metal military vehicle models have been produced for quite some time but because of cost and weight, no doubt, they have been confined to nothing much over 1:76 scale.

Normally produced in a centrifugal casting machine, the type model soldiers are cast in, white metal model vehicle kits are more expensive than those cast in resin or plastic. White metal railway locomotive kits have been available for some time, and the majority suffered from the same faults – bad mould-making producing ill-fitting and distorted castings which have proved difficult to fit together. However, with careful mould-making a good model is possible.

Kit design in white metal is important because the final assembly has one major minus factor – weight! White metal is very heavy and models made up in this material (especially butt-jointed, slab-sided pieces) are rather hefty and a little unwieldy when assembled.

There are three kits cast in white metal made by the Scale Link company (who also manufacture model railway accessories) to 1:32 scale and are all based on World War One subjects – a Rolls Royce armoured car, a Renault FT17 tank and a British 60pdr field gun. The vehicles and gun are designed to be in scale with the company's 1:32 scale range of World War One model soldiers and equipment.

Soldered construction is recommended for white metal kits: it not only produces a stronger model but also enables any distorted parts to be bent into shape to fit. If one joint is secured previously, the part can be bent against a soldered joint, whereas with a glued joint this would not really be possible.

Skytrex and Platoon 20 produce 1:76 scale white metal kits of modern battle tanks. These are similar in construction and design to resin kits and are more expensive.

More kits are planned in white metal by Scale Link at the time of writing, possibly with the introduction of more etched metal parts to replace some of the white metal bits. It will be interesting to see more kits in etched brass, though so far as is known only one at present exists, a Renault FT17 by a French manufacturer. Photo-etched brass or nickel silver kits would be a boon to the military vehicle modeller but it seems that, once again, the properties of this medium have been more fully developed by model railway kit makers. Verlinden, however, have released a set of mesh armour to fit Tamiya's 1:35 scale M113 armoured personnel carrier to convert it to the Israeli 'Zelda'.

Card Models

Card should not be dismissed as an out-moded material. True, plastic card has eclipsed it for construction work but the author remembers some excellent models usually built as part of dioramas by the late John Sandars. John would build models not produced by the major kit manufacturers in card, plastic, wood, resin castings, wire, etc. In fact, everything that he could adapt, he did. John's work still exists in the British Model Soldier Society's collection as inspiration to all and a special category of competition class for dioramas is named after him and forms part of the British Model Soldier Society's Annual Competitions, a fitting tribute to a pioneer military vehicle modeller.

Card cut-out models do exist for military vehicles and it's

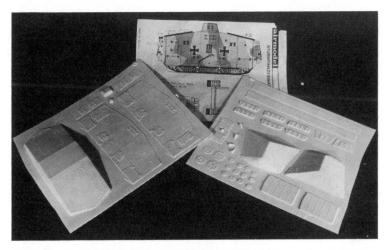

Still on the plastic theme, this WW1 German AF7V tank is vac-formed from plastic sheet by the German Airmodel company to 1:35 scale. Vac-forms need a little experience.

surprising that some enterprising manufacturer has not fully developed the theme. However, pre-printed plastic card sheets are available from Japan with conversion parts ready marked out for the vehicle kit modeller.

BASIC KIT ASSEMBLY

Plastic vehicle kits, like soldier kits, need a fair amount of care and attention to achieve good results. Beginners can produce a fine model with their first attempt but with a lot of tyro modellers the opposite is often the case.

The most important point is never rush it! Take your time. It's fairly obvious we all want to see a collection of parts in a box transformed quickly into a work of art. While a model should not take a lifetime to construct, it should not be hurried to the point of ruin.

What follows are some pointers and advice for novices on plastic kit construction. It is difficult to generalise because individual model vehicles are nearly all different, but these tips are offered from quite a few year's kit building 'under the belt.'

When you first open the kit box, do not remove any of the parts from their runners or sprues but leave them in place and read the instruction sheets before you do anything else. It is

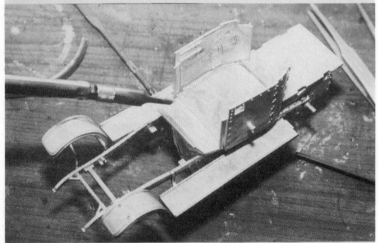

Photographs on these pages show stages in the construction of a 1:32 white metal WW1 Rolls-Royce armoured car from a Scale Link kit. Opposite, top, cleaning the parts with a glass fibre pencil, centre soldering parts, bottom the assembled vehicle showing the etched brass wheel spoking. Above, airbrushing with a Badger 100 GXF airbrush and weathering in process, using Carr's brush-applied weathering powders.

difficult, granted, to keep your hands off the moulded detailed components, but you should only examine them after complete familiarisation with the instruction sheet.

Identify each 'group' of parts on its runner. Some manufacturers are good and group them while others do not, which can result in an impractical layout. Next, check everything is there. Laborious, yes, but imagine getting half way through building the model and you find a part is missing. There's nothing more certain to make a modeller lose his temper than a missing part. It rarely happens today but is not unknown.

The ever-present mould release agents will be found on the surfaces of the kit parts, plus 'human grease' from handling, so it's advisable to wash everything, still on the runners, in warm soapy water. Household washing up liquid is ideal for this. Soak the kit parts for about 15 minutes then remove, rinse thoroughly with cold water and allow to dry out naturally.

After washing it's better to cut down the handling of kit parts to the absolute minimum and only when they're needed for assembly. When removing parts from the runners do not twist them until they are free, but cut them away with a sharp knife on a hard surface or with a pair of single edge cutters. Remove any mould part lines with a knife edge and fine abrasive. Polish up the part using 'Scotchbrite' for an extra special finish. This can't be used on too small parts as they would probably become trapped within its open fibres, but on large parts it's ideal.

Wherever possible use liquid cement for construction and apply it sparingly. Remember that 'cement' is a solvent and it

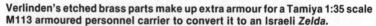

Verlinden's etched brass parts make up extra armour for a Tamiya 1:35 scale M113 armoured personnel carrier to convert it to an Israeli *Zelda*.

melts the plastic, so be very careful with it on small parts.

Follow the manufacturer's instructions for assembly and only when you have a few models behind you should you adapt constructional methods to your own sequences. Also, as you progress, check the model against any published references. Any deviations could be corrected if they are of a minor nature during construction. Major mistakes will, more often than not, entail equally major corrective measures. Finally, give the model the 'once over' and fill any gaps with body putty. Next another washing process should be made to get rid of any grease on the surface which will probably inhibit paint adhesion.

Use a soft brush and wash the model, or alternatively soak the whole thing in warm water and mild detergent, rinse and allow to dry. This action will also get rid of any dust, plastic and natural. Avoid rubbing the plastic surface after washing because this will build up static and attract more dust particles.

PAINTING

Painting the model is one of the most enjoyable parts of the constructional sequence. This is just as well, as there is nothing worse than leaving an unpainted vehicle on display showing all the warts of the construction stages. This does not mean that the paintwork should cover a multitude of sins, including bad workmanship! Whether you use a brush or spray, the overall aim should be for a good even coverage without runs or imperfections.

Brush painting will be the course taken by most modellers and the first point with vehicle modelling is to use a brush to suit the size of the model. You will not get good paint coverage on a 1:35 scale vehicle with a 00 size brush, just as using a No. 6 on a 1:76 scale tankette would be overdoing things somewhat. As with figure modelling, use the best quality of brush you can afford; sables are best, and just because the model is a tank it doesn't mean the work has to be 'slap-dash'. Cheap brushes do not last and they always seem to shed hairs where and when you don't want them to.

Mix the paint well, whether enamel or acrylic, and ensure that the consistency is correct. Decant the paint into a palette-type dish if you wish, but don't rush the task, and apply the paint in a succession of thin coats rather than one thick one. This statement is repeated throughout the book but try it once and you'll really notice the difference.

Keep the brush strokes even and draw the brush in one direction only, allowing the paint to cover evenly. Do not brush over areas you have just painted and always allow paint to dry out thoroughly before overpainting. Avoid using small brushes on large areas which will only leave plenty of brush marks and not give a suitable maximum coverage.

Two or multi-tone camouflage patterns should be within the talents of most modellers. However, those that are sprayed on, such as modern United States army and German WW2 schemes, are best done with an airbrush. So, at first stick to single colour finishes or multi-coloured patterns which are brush applied on the real vehicle.

No comment will be made here on what the so-called 'correct' colours to paint military vehicles are. Far too much time and energy and lots of hot air have been expended on trying to prove how 'correct' a colour is. Ask any serviceman, past or present, and you'll probably get the same answer – "they were all different." Time and weather alters colours and the human eye does not always interpret colour correctly. If you choose a colour, rely on the manufacturers' mix – it will be near enough, or near as anyone needs – despite what the self-styled 'experts' try to tell everyone.

Spray Painting

Spraying, especially by airbrush and when done correctly, does produce a superior finish to that of the conventional paintbrush, and even more so on larger scale models. Larger scale models can be painted with the many aerosol canned paints available. The major paint makers offer these in all the popular military colours so it's possible to obtain the ones you need fairly easily.

The model's surfaces to be sprayed must be scrupulously clean and the spraying done in a well-ventilated area. This does not necessarily mean out of doors because even the slightest breeze will deflect the spray's mist from its intended path. Also, ensure that any overspray does not, or cannot, settle on nearby areas. A large cardboard box with one side cut away is a good extemporised spray booth and, if you wish to buy the real thing, 3M do a version in expanded polystyrene.

Simple display. Tamiya's 1:35 scale US Army M.U.T.T. displayed on a wooden base with groundwork from Milliput textured with a toothbrush!

When spraying with aerosols you have little or no control over pressure, so keep the can at least a foot away from the model, further if possible. Do not be impatient but cover the subject in several light coats. Do not begin spraying directly at the model but aim to one side then press the button and move across the model, from side to side, only releasing the supply when you've passed the model completely. The spray must be kept parallel in its movement to the model's surface. Do not, under any circumstances spray at an angle or haphazardly with aerosol can sprays, or attempt to 'spot' spray any areas with a direct burst onto the model's surface. This will result in thick blobs of paint in one area.

During spraying try wherever possible to mount the model on some form of base that can be moved easily to enable all areas to be sprayed. A block of wood is suitable so long as it's big enough not to topple over and can be reached easily to turn the model round.

Aerosol paint sprays are only good enough for covering the model with one colour, unless, of course, a hard-edged camouflage pattern is needed. Then only by masking off areas of the base colour with masking film can the second colour be sprayed on.

Try experimenting with different-sized holes cut in a piece of card and held in front of the aerosol spray to reduce the area coverage. Good results and fair representations of sprayed mottled camouflage effects can be made by this method, but it needs a lot of care and attention and lots of practice to make it work properly without a lot of paint spatter.

Airbrushes

The airbrush is an expensive piece of equipment, but, once mastered, the modeller will wonder how he or she had managed without it in the first place.

Airbrushes need expertise in use and lots of practice is recommended for good results. However, there are cheaper types of airbrush available that are infinitely more flexible and better than aerosol spray paint cans. Although the simpler airbrushes are still powered by aerosols they offer a finer spray and some degree of spray control. It is, perhaps, better to begin with a cheaper instrument and then graduate to one of the more expensive models.

Airbrushes come in different types, although they all produce the same basic result. Terms such as single and double action simply describe the method of paint and air control on the instrument. Double action brushes are controlled from one lever/button – press down for air and move the control back and forth for paint supply. All this is controlled by one finger. Single action types have a press-down for air and paint delivery. The actual amount of paint is regulated by a movable nut acting on the airbrush's needle control.

Outside and inside mix brushes are also available. The outside mix types are usually single action and the paint is supplied from an outside mounted reservoir and mixed with the air supply outside the instrument's body. Inside mix means just that; the air and paint are atomized inside the body and released via the nozzle.

More and more modellers are using airbrushes and the results speak for themselves. This book is, however, for beginners and the purchase of an airbrush is not recommended, except for the really affluent, in the first stages of interest in the hobby, where other more important purchases are required. Graduate to the air-brush via conventional painting with a brush.

Decals or Transfers

Waterslide decals (or transfers as they used to be known) are usually a minimal part of any plastic vehicle kit, military vehicles not having a lot of 'decoration' such as found on some aircraft.

Rub-down types of decal, exactly the same as dry lettering rub-down print, Letraset, Chartpak, etc., are not usually supplied but they can be found in the lists of the many accessories manufacturers who advertise in model magazines. These decals are infinitely superior to the waterslide types, but more expensive.

Waterslide types are easy to use. Never soak them until saturated, but only wet them enough to release the decal from the backing. Apply them directly to the surface, position and blot dry, ensuring there are no air bubbles present. Where possible use a wetting agent which softens the decal enabling it to follow the contours of any uneven surface, such as rivets. Waterslide decals stick better to gloss surfaces, and do not go down well on matt paint finishes. An application of gloss varnish in the areas of the decal can be made, the transfer applied and, when dried out, oversprayed with matt varnish. Decal carrier film is always glossy to some degree, even if the decals are listed as matt. Therefore, cut all decals out with a sharp scalpel blade and ensure you just skim the colour of the decal itself.

Weathering

Weathering is representing in miniature the effects of the elements on a painted surface. This can be loosely defined as fading, chipping and discoloration of paintwork; oil, grease and fuel stains with dust and mud splashes are also candidates. It must not be overdone, however, as nothing looks worse than badly done weathering! Applied in a haphazard manner nothing could be further from the fidelity to subject the modeller is trying to create. When weathering military vehicles, err on the side of light-handedness and try to represent, realistically, fair wear and tear.

One school of thought in vehicle painting favours a 'graduated' application of colour. Beginning with a base colour, successive coats are applied using the base colour to which is added a trace of white or a lighter tone. This shade is overpainted, but not overall, in the areas where depth is suggested by natural features, such as panel lines, raised

Conversion of an Italeri kit into the German WW2 Sdkfz 234/3 armoured car. Simple, but very effective, scenic work on the base completes the model.

angle irons, rivets, etc. This provides an 'artistically-weathered' appearance on the model but it does need a lot of practice to be convincing. It can be done with both paintbrush and airbrush. Weathering will come with practice. Like painting model soldiers, it is difficult to describe but easy to copy when demonstrated.

Powders are another useful medium. Use either powdered pastel chalks, obtained by rubbing the sticks on glasspaper to produce the powder, or powders sold for weathering models. The latter are finely ground powders with a slightly waxy texture which enables them to adhere to the model's surface. Carr's Modelling Products produce such powders in many different colours. Powders work especially well on vehicles intended for a desert environment, representing dust and sand, and can be brushed onto upper surfaces to collect in a natural manner.

Dry Brushing

Dry brushing techniques are an important contribution to making weathered finishes. Dry brushing is easy and best carried out with an old paintbrush – at least a No. 5 size is best and the fluffier the bristles the better.

The brush is dipped in the paint only about 1mm – 2mm deep on the bristles and brushed to and fro over tissue to remove most of the paint. It is then lightly flicked over the model so that any raised detail receives a 'highlighting'. Again, do not overdo it, and keep everything low key. Do not, for instance, dry brush a model with white paint – it looks unreal and, frankly, awful. It is better to mix the base colour with a lot of white to obtain a highlight, and use that instead.

DISPLAY BASES

Whenever possible, make a base on which to mount your model. It need not be elaborate but it should be neat and presentable with, perhaps, a nameplate with the vehicle's description. It is far easier to handle a baseplate than the model, especially if you've spent many hours on it. Dependent on the size of your model make sure that the base is not too big, but also ensure that no parts of the model, such as gun barrels, overhang the base.

Attach the model to the base so that it will not move or, worse still, fall off when handled. The most secure method is not, as is universally thought and done, to glue the model directly to the base but to secure it with a nut and bolt. Also, if you included groundwork on your base make sure the vehicle 'sits' into it, especially if it's a tank. Remember, you're

Cut-away kit conversions are good fun. This is Kelvin Barber's 1:48 scale Bandai Tiger II conversion.

representing an armoured, heavy vehicle in miniature so its tracks should not be shown perched on blades of grass!

The nut should be attached to the underside of the model. On tanks this is no problem and easily done during construction by drilling a hole in the hull bottom then gluing (use epoxy resin for strength) the nut inside the hull over the hole so it can receive the bolt passed through a hole drilled in the base and up into the model. If you put any terrain on the base ensure that it is level, otherwise you will have to alter the position of the vehicle's suspension to follow the groundwork. This must be done early in the constructional stage, so think ahead. The nut and bolt will still work with uneven groundwork although the bolt hole may need to be drilled at an angle to locate and match up perfectly. Always ensure the bolt head is countersunk in the bottom of the base – for obvious reasons.

The base itself can be made up from laminate-faced chipboard with iron-on edging or, for a more attractive job, edged with picture framing or decorative beading, mitre-jointed at the corners and glued and pinned in place.

Superdetailing

Once you have mastered kit construction, you will, no doubt, graduate to adding extra details. These may take the form of crew's personal equipment or replacing solid moulded parts

Simple conversion of Tamiya's KV1. Hull details involve replacement of trackguard supports and a stowage bin added. Trackguards have been distorted slightly. A new turret has been built from plastic card but utilises parts from the kit's cast turret which show up darker on the scratchbuilt turret. With the scratchbuilt turret in place, the model is ready for painting.

A major conversion in 1:35 scale on Airfix's Bedford anti-tank gun portee. The General Service and Trooper variants have scratchbuilt bodies and cab tops vac-formed from plastic card and virtually undistinguishable from the original 'cabless' kit.

such as handrails with ones from wire or heat-stretched plastic. Any heavily moulded details look better if replaced with an in-scale part. Also, the parts that are the wrong shape, or have been left off due to the complexity, should be built up from scratch, and the model will be all the better for it. This procedure is known as superdetailing and is the first step in converting plastic vehicle kits.

CONVERSIONS

Converting plastic vehicle kits, whether it is a minor or major conversion, is a satisfying exercise. Again, leave more ambitious conversions until later and begin with something easy, such as a turret replacement, or the up-gunning of a tank. This way, if your efforts don't come up to expectations you have not irrevocably destroyed any parts of the kit.

First, a scale drawing will be needed or, alternatively, base the conversion on photographs if no drawing is available. You can produce your own drawings to scale for the parts which will make up the changes.

Conversions can be effected by cross-kitting, i.e. mixing of different parts of the same type of vehicle as made by

Extensive conversion of Tamiya's M4A3 into the M4A2 early variant involves a completely scratchbuilt hull and modifications to the kit turret. This conversion by the author is an ideal beginner's model.

different kit manufacturers. The US Sherman tank variants are a prime case where cross-kitting can produce different sub-marks of the basic vehicle. Often the mixing of parts from different makes of kit can be made to work very well, especially with World War Two types.

With plastic card, a scale drawing and plenty of ingenuity, the conversion of commercial kits is a satisfying pursuit, as is the research and planning that go together to lay the basis of the actual alterations necessary.

SCRATCHBUILDING

It is difficult to define just where the dividing line between converted and scratchbuilt lies. With all scales, modellers tend to use available parts such as road wheels, tracks and 'standard' types of running gear parts. This is different from the true definition of every part being built entirely from scratch.

However, guided by competitions, it could be judged that if the complete bodywork of a model was built from scratch using, say, only the wheels and tracks on a tank – or the wheels alone on a truck or car – it could loosely be termed

Scratchbuilt WW1 British staff car displayed on a simple scenic base. The fingers give some idea of this minute model's size in 1:76 scale.

scratch built. It certainly could not be called a conversion. Hence the difficulty in drawing a definite line between the two.

Research is all-important. As much information as possible should be accrued. It cannot be said too often that you must exhaust every avenue of approach for information, both written and illustrative. Do not attempt a model on meagre information alone unless, of course, you are satisfied that no further information is available. Then and only then will you have to do some intelligent guesswork and make a start. Many times modellers have produced work from virtually nothing in the way of reference, only to find that 'someone' has been sitting on the material they have so sorely needed. Obviously, there is nothing that can be done in such a situation, but remember to smile if it happens to you, especially if some 'expert' pulls your model apart – verbally – at a club meeting or in a competition. At least you learn from the experience!

Use the model press to have your requests printed for information. It usually costs nothing to have a 'please help' notice printed either in the news or letters columns and usually does bring in very good results from helpful modellers.

Plastic card (polystyrene sheet) is a superb medium for scratchbuilding purposes, being easy to work and pleasant to use when compared with card and wood. Seemingly complex parts become an easy exercise using plastic card and quite difficult shapes are made easier by the very nature of the material. It is easily scored and snapped, which is preferable to cutting right through; it can be moulded fairly easily with home-produced plug moulds, heat formed into circular structures; and, of course, it needs no special adhesives other than polystyrene cement, the liquid variety being by far the most suitable.

Scratchbuilders can vacu-form it into quite complex shapes if they possess one of the rare Mattel vac-forming machines, now unfortunately taken off the market, but once a great boon to modellers. Vac-forming can be done commercially by various companies, but you may have to place an order for a lot of parts.

Commercial kit parts are also used extensively and copied by home moulding techniques, which technically is an illegal practice. However, it would be very difficult to prove unless of course some 'enterprising' body began manufacture with the idea of selling the product. Court cases have arisen over plagiarism of model soldiers but none are known for anyone home-moulding commercial plastic kit parts for their own use. Some books and magazine articles even advocate the practice which appears to be, by convention, a widely accepted method of modelling.

Ken Musgrave's scratchbuilt Vickers Medium Mk. 1A* in 1:32 scale.

Moulding rubbers are now widely available and all military modellers should have a go at moulding their own bits and pieces. They are especially helpful to the military vehicle builder in that he need only produce one master part to cast multitudes from. So handy when building the running gear of a tank – especially when you can't use or adapt any commercial parts.

The term RTV applied to moulding rubbers means that the rubber cures at room temperature (*Room Temperature Vulcanising*). A catalyst is added to the silicone rubber, mixed in and the rubber is poured into the mould and left to cure. Silicone rubber will mould the finest of detail and really must be tried by the modeller to ascertain its properties. Alec Tiranti produces a very useful little booklet telling all you need to know about producing moulds from silicone rubbers and suitable casting materials. It is recommended that it be obtained and its methods put into practice.

Do not think that scratchbuilding a tank or truck is beyond your skills. Granted, your first finished scale model may not be your idea of the real subject in miniature. Its fidelity to prototype may be suspect but at least you will have 'made it yourself'.

Whatever the scale you choose to model in, try to stick to an easy subject first time round. You may find you're capable of a more complicated model, if so be guided by what you feel you can achieve within your skill range.

The majority of tank hulls are square structures, with lots of right-angled joints. Even today's advanced battle tanks are a basic box construction, despite any additional armours, panniers, add-on equipment and such like mounted over or attached to this basic shape. So, before you begin, ascertain those basic shapes of hull and turret and work out how you will achieve the shapes.

If you decide to model a vehicle where a scale drawing is available, take off the measurements for all parts that make up the hull, using all views and allowing for any angled pieces. If the drawing is a different scale from the one you normally work in these measurements should be scaled up or down onto your own plan. Use graph paper for easy transfer and a pocket calculator to check your measurements. You should end up with a collection of drawings or templates of all the major components to the scale in which you're modelling. All that's left is to transfer these to plastic card.

Ensure that you allow for any plastic card thicknesses and which parts will butt joint over or inside others.

Assembly should be made on a completely flat surface. A piece of thick glass is ideal to set up all the cut-out parts on and is also useful for cutting out on. Begin by fitting the hull sides to the floor and then all the parts, making up the engine deck front and rear armour plate. Use a square to ensure everything is correctly positioned and an adjustable square for any angles. On larger scale models internal bracing or bulkheads may be necessary, so put these in at the preliminary stages. Also decide if you are to have an open turret ring on the hull top. If so, this should be cut out of the part with a compass cutter *before* the whole part is removed from the plastic sheet.

If the turret is made up from flat plates it can be built up just as the hull was. If it is a cast type, two methods are possible. In small scales it can be carved from wood, sanded and finished, or shaped from laminated sheets of plastic card. For the larger scales a wooden master can be carved and the turret plug moulded.

Plug moulding is where a master former is pushed through previously heated plastic card pinned securely to a piece of wood over a hole having the same outline shape as the master former. The master is plunged quickly and firmly through the hole, where the heated plastic card is formed around it. Shapes which curve in under the turret wall to the ring (undercuts) should be made as two-part formers. They can be bolted together for shaping for accuracy then parted and used as separate plug moulds. Turrets in 1:35 scale can be made this way. If at first the plug does not go through the hole cleanly, reheat the plastic and try again. A domestic oven hotplate or grill is ideal for softening the card. Wear gloves to protect the hands when plug moulding.

Roadwheels wherever possible should be used from kits, or adapted. Likewise, the trackwork can be used and adapted. If nothing is available, however, you'll have to scratchbuild. Wheels can be built up from discs and 'washers' cut from plastic card with a compass cutter. The ideal method is to produce as near perfect a master as you can, then make a mould of the part in RTV silicone rubber, from which identical castings can be made. This goes for the idlers and sprockets and any return rollers too – make one pattern and cast many, as it would be tedious to make each

Scratchbuilding often entails moulding your own parts. This is a two-piece mould made for a part by the author using Tiranti's RTV31 rubber. The £1 coin gives an indication of the size.

wheel individually, considering the amount needed for the average armoured vehicle.

Trackwork is not too difficult to scratchbuild. Simple plate tracks are no real problem but skeleton-type tracks need a lot more expertise and a lot of care, especially in the larger scales. A master can be made up from plastic card of about six links in length. Also make one or two individual links which will be needed to form around the idler and sprocket wheels. Make a two-part mould which will enable the teeth to be included also. Cast the track in 'runs' and fit these to the model. Polyester resin will give good results, but polyurethane resin is superb for tank tracks.

The track master must have perfectly square ends when you make it, otherwise any castings produced will not lie

The late John Sandar's Bren gun carrier completely scratchbuilt in cardboard and wood with heavily converted figures.

straight over the roadwheels and will twist out of true when glued in place. Working tracks and suspensions are something else, and beyond the scope of this basic discussion on scratch-building scale military vehicles.

Trucks, cars and other softskin vehicles can be, in the majority of cases, a little more difficult to scratchbuild, especially if they have many compound curves, such as wings, bonnets, hoods, and the like. This is especially so for civilian models adapted or pressed into military service. Vehicles built specifically for the military tend to have more angular lines and are much simpler shapes overall.

Again, kit parts, and especially wheels, are most useful, but the scratchbuilding of these items and casting copies off is recommended. Tyres are made in standard sizes so a range of tyre masters could be made up as you progress, as can the wheels and hubs. Masters, using the compass cutter, can be made up from laminations of plastic card. The tread is another matter and needs thought. Fortunately, unlike the fine slots in civilian tyres most military tyres have huge track-grip treads so it's not impossible to cut a passable representation of the tyre tread on your master. A two-piece RTV silicone mould will give many castings.

Rounded wings can be plug-moulded in plastic card from wooden formers or a pattern carved from the solid and then moulded up. The inside of the mould is then lined with thin wax and the other half of the mould poured to form a 'shell'. This takes experimentation and works well with the new

Instructional model of a Landing Craft Tank (Armoured) from the Imperial War Museum with two Centaurs (close support tanks) and a Sherman on board.

polyurethane plastic resins which pour much better than the polyester types for this type of mould.

Cabs, bodies and suchlike are similar in construction to the basic 'squared' tank hulls but a chassis will need care to ensure it is perfectly true. Chassis can be built up from Plastruct sections where the channel-shaped sections are readily available, especially for larger scales.

There is a lot more work in the average truck than many modellers expect, because much of it is visible – the supports between the chassis and body, fuel tanks, brake linkages, differential bell-housings, chassis cross-members and supports, and much more. Look at any truck and you will appreciate what needs doing.

Scratchbuilding is something all modellers should aspire to – it is, perhaps, the most rewarding part of military modelling.

6 DIORAMAS

The word diorama covers a broad canvas of modelling, from open-type miniature scenic settings on bases to ingeniously-lit boxed dioramas, or shadow boxes as they're also known. Another word associated with models in scenic settings is 'vignette'. This term is found in competition rules and usually means up to a maximum of three figures on a scenically-dressed base, though you won't find this description explained in any dictionary!

Dioramas fall into two categories, open and boxed, the former being viewable from any side, plane or angle, whereas the latter normally only allow the viewer to see what the builder wants him to from one viewpoint. It will come as no surprise to discover that open dioramas are, therefore, more commonly encountered than boxed types. The latter do require a certain expertise and, more often than not, artificial lighting to create an atmosphere within.

At the time of writing there is a book in print titled *How to Build Dioramas* by Shepherd Paine, who is a master of the art. This book should be sought out, read and then read again. It is an absolute mine of information and although it does not exclusively cover pure military dioramas, they do make up most of its content. Even though it is written by an American for an American readership, and thus some of the terms and materials may be strange to readers in other countries, this does not lessen the book's appeal with its excellent design and the knowledge and methods for diorama building passed on by the author.

Planning
Planning is an all-important consideration for the diorama builder. First, the most successful dioramas tell a story which needs only the minimum wordage on a descriptive label. Also, balance is very important in any diorama, open or

Resin moulded accessory for diorama builders, painted and dry brushed ready for incorporating into the diorama. This is a gun position with gabions (stone and earth-filled baskets) as a defensive wall.

boxed, as a base that is too large with figures congregating in the centre destroys all illusions.

A small overcrowded base will have the same effect. Therefore, planning means just that – a story line, good composition, correct base size centred on the model or models involved, scale ratio and, above all, good modelling to complete the scene in miniature.

Boxed dioramas are governed by the same parameters, but internal manipulation and lighting must produce a good effect, so planning is even more important. It is wise to make a 'model of the model to be built' – in this case a simple composition built up from cardboard will suffice – plus lots of sketches to enable the correct positions of the models to be established inside. As always, take plenty of time in the planning stage to map out exactly what you wish to convey.

Lighting

Boxed dioramas can show outdoor scenes but usually, because of their very direct and enclosed construction, depict interior scenes where all the lighting and shadow effects can be adjusted by the builder to the best advantage.

The outer box should contain the inner scene inside it, forming its own box with the interior angles arranged to convince the viewer's eye that that what he sees is all perfectly composed and symmetrical. Walls, for instance, must be so shaped that perspective appears correct, even though it it isn't due to foreshortening because of depth limitation. A lot of modellers employ different scales of figures to produce subtle perspective effects which help to cement the illusion firmly in the viewer's mind.

Treatment for a typical resin or plaster moulding, a ruined stone wall. First paint black or dark grey all over.

Dab on ochre and green patches, using a piece of sponge or foam plastic.

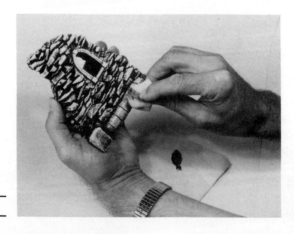

Highlight with white mixed with the other colours – plain white is too bright and surface texture detail will not be seen.

The finished piece has depth and is now ready for use in a diorama.

Lighting is not complicated but is definitely experimental to the point of being set up by mainly trial and error. It can be supplied from an overhead low wattage strip light or from various angles via miniature bulbs powered by batteries or a transformer supply. Just as for set-ups for a real live stage show or play the lighting must be adjusted until the effect is exactly what the modeller is seeking. No two dioramas will ever be exactly the same and each individual will require a different, often a wholly different, approach to illumination.

Fibre optics can play a great part in miniature illumination and effects, and offer a reasonably-priced medium for experiment. Fibre optics consists of acrylic fibres of various diameters, from virtually a 'hair' to about 2mm – 3mm diameter, which will transmit light throughout their lengths from one single light source. Acrylic rod in the Plastruct ABS plastic range will work similarly for larger displays. The fibre optic works, because of its molecular structure, by transmitting light along its length. Place a light source at one end of a piece of fibre, which can then remain straight or be bent into any shape or direction, and that light source, whatever its colour, will appear at the other end of the fibre. By cutting the ends to different angles, different effects can be obtained.

Coloured lights are possible too by placing a coloured

View inside a boxed diorama of a German warship's boiler room in 54mm scale by Hecker and Goros.

screen (a coloured cellophane chocolate sweet wrapper works!) between the bulb and the end of the fibre. The muzzle flash of small arms caught at the moment of discharge, lights on vehicles and their instrument panels, candles, torches and fires, to list but a few effects, can be very realistically depicted with fibre optic.

A one-piece diorama base, cast in plaster. Pelikan Plaka water-based paint was used here. Note the extensive dry brushing.

Buy a pack and experiment yourself. Who knows, modellers are innovators and you may discover something nobody has thought of doing.

Earthwork

Top dressing for groundwork from natural materials is easy to collect, grade and prepare for use in diorama work. At the side of the road or driveway at your home a lot of 'dust' collects at the edges, thrown there by vehicles. This natural 'scatter' material is easily scooped up into a container and sifted through a cheap plastic tea-strainer which will eliminate a lot of the bigger bits, such as small pebbles inadvertently included. However, smaller pebbles do have their uses so don't throw them away; they can be used in certain model environments, such as where a lot of ground surface damage has been made by shelling or earthworks dug and where small rocks will have been blown or shovelled to the surface.

Nothing looks more distracting than small natural pebbles 'balanced' on the groundwork or pushed into it with little surround ridges formed. Avoid this at all costs – the 'perching' of pebbles on the groundwork to represent rocks and their incorporation into the terrain really separates the 'absolute mess' from the model. If you model such terrain,

Diorama formed from commercial unmodified parts from the Preiser range is still effective.

mix the pebbles well into your groundwork foundation material, rather like currants into a cake mix!

Never, under any circumstances, leave natural terrain materials unpainted. They may look good off the diorama or in their own environment but, when the models are added, they take on an unreal appearance. It may appear a contradiction in terms to treat natural material with unnatural toning down procedures to look 'natural' but it must be done. The natural material forms the texture, not necessarily the colour. Paint and drybrush the surface texture just as you would any unnatural materials.

Materials for the actual groundwork and contouring are many and varied. For small areas epoxy putty, such as Milliput, is ideal but its cost denies its use on any grand scale. Das Pronto self-hardening modelling clay, which needs no firing, can be sculptured very easily with simple modelling tools. Large areas are best covered with a plaster mix or Polyfilla in either powder or ready-mixed form. Tetrion is tougher and more textured and good for rock and stonework. Before laying down fillers onto a solid diorama base score the base with a cross-hatched pattern to enable the groundwork material to adhere. Mix in some colour too, powder or water colour, and preferably a dark one such as deep brown, so that if any cracks appear during drying they will not show a garish white. Also, with top cover in place, plaster in its virgin state becomes difficult to paint. Try mixing very fine sand in with the Polyfilla for a textured finish. Some PVA glue added to the mixture will help 'bind' it and produce a more durable ground cover.

Grass

Grass, both long and short varieties, is found in practically every environment, from lush green to the scorched stubby variety.

For finely clipped, short grass the model hobby trade came up with a very good 'substitute' some years ago called 'static' or 'Streu' grass, or Noch, which is a trade name. Manufactured in Germany, the 'mix' consists of very fine, individual nylon flock hairs, 2mm – 3mm long. The material is scattered evenly from a 'puffer pack' over a previously glued area – PVA glue is best because it dries transparent – and the excess is blown away, which causes the individual 'hairs' to stand erect. When all is completely dry, painting and

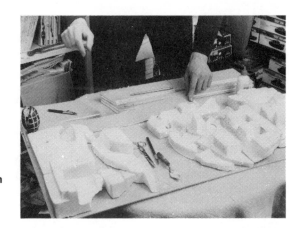

Planning terrain in a diorama using expanded polystyrene.

Covering the terrain with water-soluble plaster bandage and plaster filler.

Ground scatter material being applied over wet plaster to make a stream bed.

Bristles and split cane have many uses in dioramas. The bristles at right will make fine long grass.

weathering must be done, because as supplied, static grass is a little gaudy in colour and can look unnatural over a large area.

Static grass is available already stuck down on brown paper sheets or in rolls to be glued down on flat surfaces. Gentle curves are possible but any bumpy terrain needs a little adjusting over the contours. Again, it needs painting to tone it down somewhat.

Instructional model built by the author of a Roman Milecastle has static grass around the walls and shaded after the glue had set.

Resin cast roof sections painted and dry-brushed.

For 'clumps' of grass on the static grass areas add some chopped dyed plastic cellular foam, universally referred to as 'foam rubber'. This material, available commercially, is very good for representing foliage also. It is on sale in model shops, usually packed in plastic bags.

Long grass is a little more difficult to reproduce convincingly. Sisal or hemp rope or string are two good substitutes. The former must be boiled first to remove the

Diorama by Barry Reynolds with a scenic backdrop in place during photography. The figures are Historex.

Small diorama which tells a story – 'Surrounded'. Good composition gives this scene a sense of urgency.

size added, then stretched under weight before unwinding and cutting to manageable single-fibre lengths. Then it should be dyed a dark green if required using natural or chemical dyes obtainable from hardware stores.

Unwound ropes and strings provide the stalks of long grass which are 'inserted' into patches of PVA glue. Do not drill holes and push in clumps of the string, for nothing looks worse or less real. Work on small areas at a time if a large expanse is to be covered and cover it bit-by-bit until all is in place. This way the grass will stand until the glue sets. When all is dry trim with nail scissors for an even or uneven finish. Paint and drybrush for effect.

Experiment with bristles from old brushes too, and always be on the lookout for new and not-so-obvious substitutes for grass.

Water

Making imitation water is surrounded by a lot of mystique and so-called 'difficulties'. Most of this is unfounded and modelling water is very easy to do in scenic settings.

The easiest and most basic, yet still very convincing, method is varnish. All that's needed to represent running water are two or three coats of a good quality, clear polyurethane varnish, brushed on a previously painted surface, such as plaster, whether smooth or rough. The convincing touch lies in the colours that are painted on to represent the water. Remember, water isn't always, or rather doesn't always appear, blue. Again, environment is important and this should be ironed out in the planning stages.

Never use glass to represent water on dioramas that can be moved or held to be viewed. It may be fine for a fixed location but glass is dangerous and breaks easily, often with disastrous results on contact with human skin. Many modellers will insist on using glass when clear acrylic sheet (Perspex or Plexiglass) is available. Although more expensive than glass, acrylic is more adaptable and ripples can be

Water made from resin with floating leaves looks realistic in this painted diorama accessory casting. Such parts can form the centrepiece of a diorama.

formed on its surface with acrylic gel or liquid intended for using with paints. Acrylic can also be spaced over a stream or river bed for greater illusion of depth. Also, you can paint its undersurface for effect.

Clear casting resins are now used quite a lot to represent water and are very easy to mix and apply. All you need to ensure is that a natural barrier must be in place to stop the resin 'creeping' where it shouldn't. Resins will tend to 'creep' upwards on terrain which destroys any illusion, particularly on river banks. So, if possible, model the banks, dock walls or whatever *over* the edges of the resin. Alternatively, make the water off the diorama and add it as a one-piece moulding later. Form the area of water on a flat, but well-greased (Vaseline or any petroleum jelly will do) surface. When set, any surface tackiness can be removed with acetone – or use ladies' nail polish remover.

For water with a choppy or rough surface pour the resin onto slightly crumpled aluminium foil and proceed as for calm water, using the surface nearest the foil as the finished model. However, ensure that your waves are 'in scale' to the model; a choppy surface is required, not a line of 'tidal waves'.

Resins can be coloured, so there is plenty of scope here. Also, they can be 'layered', allowing each successive coat to

Scale Link's cast white metal tree trunks and branches.

dry, for depth and at each layer vegetation or suchlike added. Any plastic figures that are to be positioned in the water must be painted first otherwise the resin could react with them and melt the plastic.

Hedgerows and trees

Far too many modellers use far too much untreated natural lichen to represent trees and hedges on their models. Left untreated it looks . . . just like lichen. If possible leave lichen well alone, because there are better unnatural materials now available on the market.

Rubberised horsehair (hair sprayed in a rubber solution and formed into honeycombed 'blocks') as used by upholsterers is cheap and easy to work with. Finished with shredded dyed foam foliage, a good hedge, bush or tree results. All can be stuck together with PVA glue. Suitable natural twigs are easily adapted and pressed into service as tree trunks and branches or as bare trees, such as those found in winter. Keep your eyes open for any likely examples when you're out walking in the country or even when taking a stroll round the garden at home.

Fine multi-strand wire rope unwound to form trunk and branches is worth investigating. Use gloves when you handle

A diorama using flat figures and flat trees, but with a normal scenic base. Model by Mike Taylor.

Bill Evans built this attractive set-piece which includes a sizeable tree, a converted vehicle and four figures.

it, however, otherwise it is easy to cut or puncture your fingers. Once the shape is decided upon, coat with either epoxy glue or solder then skim with plaster or epoxy filler to model the bark details. Paint black and then colour and drybrush for a realistic appearance.

Foliage can either be rubberised horsehair and dyed foam stuck on or, as marketed by the American company, Woodland Scenics, an open weave mat that can be 'teased' out to shape to form foliage. White metal trunks, branches and foliage are available in the Scale Link range of scenic accessories. This company also makes photo-etched leaves and other vegetation. These are expensive but many modellers use them to effect, though without careful handling and positioning they can look a little 'mechanical'.

Remember, a mature tree is big. This should be borne in mind when a diorama is planned. A fully matured oak in 54mm scale would be massive and not really practical for a diorama, which the tree would dominate at the expense of everything else. Some form of compromise is needed.

Also, get your areas correct. The desert-type date palm tree is different from the lofty coconut South Seas palm that some modellers place incorrectly over their German WW2 Afrika Korps tanks! Refer to pictures whenever possible.

Special effects

Finally, a word about snow, a medium which seems to find great favour amongst beginners.

Model snow as an overall cover can look quite good, just as a light 'powdering' of snow can look extremely effective too. Model the stuff in plaster and paint in white, but also allow some groundwork to show here and there simply for relief of monotony if the expanse of ground is great. Wherever ridges are formed, run some salt and powdered alum (available from chemists) on these for a little light reflection of the crystals. Don't use sugar because its grains are too coarse and it dissolves after contact with water-based paints and glues.

Icicles look good on buildings and structures in winter dioramas and can be made by heat-stretching acrylic rod (ABS Plastruct range) of the clear variety and texturing it with ABS to obtain a smooth glassy surface, then varnishing to

Simple base with snow added from flour. Note how it goes over the figure's shoes.

Model in the Somerset County Museum shows 13th Somerset Light Infantry in action at Kambula against the Zulus on 29th March, 1879. Such models serve to show history in miniature and give a better understanding of how such events took place. *(Somerset County Museum).*

finish. Again, although massive icicles are often found, don't let them overpower any scene and play down their appearance as a feature.

Ice on water is best made with polyurethane varnish over a white-painted surface with a bluish tinge introduced at the edges, over which should be powdered a little 'snow' made up from white flour and powdered alum mix. Snow and ice are not a matt finish. They shine because of the crystallised water they contain so try to make your diorama 'twinkle' here and there, but don't overdo it.

Dioramas are an adventure in themselves, and should be explored fully by military modellers who should look upon them as an extension of building a single vehicle or painting a figure. When you think about it, it's a lot more fun and more satisfying to incorporate your modelling skills and output into a miniature scenic setting that perhaps represents a true event from history or the result of your own imagination coming to fruition. Happy modelling!

APPENDIX

Useful British Addresses
Alec Tiranti Ltd., 70 High Street, Theale, Reading, Berks. (Moulding rubbers and casting materials).
Strand Glassfibre, Brentway Trading Estate, Brentford, Middlesex TW8 8ER. (Moulding rubbers and casting materials).
Carr's Modelling Products, Unit 5, Centre 88 Elm Grove, Wimbledon, London SW19 4HE. (Soldering, weathering powders and scenic materials).
Hobbies, W. Hobby Ltd., Knights Hill Square, London SE27 0HH. Tools and materials mail order (and from local stockists) for the modeller.
Toolmail, 170 High Street, Lewes, East Sussex BN7 1YE. (Massive stock of tools which includes many precision types suitable for the modeller).
Proops Brothers Ltd., 52 Tottenham Court Road, London WIP OBA. (Tools and materials at competitive prices, including 'helping hands').
Applied Polymer Systems, Westburn House, 23 Parish Ghyll Road, Ilkley, West Yorkshire LS29 9NG. (Fibre optic materials).
John K. Flack, 107 Hillcrest Road., Bromley, Kent BR1 4SA. (Modelmakers' tools and materials).
Historex Agents, 3 Castle Street, Dover, Kent. (Model figure kits and accessories).

Museums
Imperial War Museum, Lambeth Road, London SE1.
National Army Museum, Hospital Road, London.
The Tank Museum, Bovington Camp, Wareham, Dorset.
A complete listing of all military museums within the United Kingdom is presented in Terry Wise's book, *A Guide to Military Museums,* published by Athena Books, 34 Imperial Crescent, Town Moor, Doncaster, South Yorkshire DN2 5BU.

Societies
British Model Soldier Society, Secretary, David Pierce, 22 Lynwood Drive, Ealing, London W5.
Miniature Armoured Fighting Vehicle Association, G. E. G. Williams, 15 Berwick Avenue, Heaton Mersey, Stockport, Cheshire SK4 3AA.

Select Bibliography

How to Build Dioramas, Shepherd Paine. Kalmbach Books. (Available from Historex Agents).
Modeling Tanks and Military Vehicles, Shepherd Paine. Kalmbach Books. (Historex).
The Verlinden Way, vols I – V, Francois Verlinden. (Available from Historex Agents).
The Modelmaker's Handbook, Albert Jackson & David Day. Pelham Books Ltd., 44 Bedford Square, London WC1B 3DU.

INDEX

OTHER MODELLING TITLES IN THE ARGUS RANGE INCLUDE:

Four-stroke Handbook	Introducing Model Aero Engines
Basic Aeromodelling	Model Aircraft Aerodynamics
Fifty Years of 'Aeromodeller'	Introducing R/C Model Aircraft
Radio Control Primer	Scale Model Aircraft for Radio Control
The Buggy Book	Building & Flying R/C Model Aircraft
The Buggy Racing Handbook	Manual of Electric R/C Cars
Boat Modelling	R/C Model Racing Cars
Handbook of Ship Modelling	Introducing R/C Model Boats
Model Yachting	R/C Fast Electric Power Boats
Radio Control in Model Boats	Introducing Model Marine Steam
Historic Ship Models	Airbrushing & Spray Painting Manual

plus many model engineering and workshop practice books

Argus Books Limited
1 Golden Square, London W1R 3AB

Send S.A.E. for latest book list